MW00879978

What an Awesome
God we serve!

Mary Syton

LESSONS
from my
CHILDREN

HOW MY CHILDREN TAUGHT ME ABOUT
THE LOVE OF GOD MY FATHER

MARY LYTTON

WESTBOW
PRESS®
A DIVISION OF THOMAS NELSON
& ZONDERVAN

Copyright © 2016 Mary Lytton.

All rights reserved. No part of this book may be used or reproduced by
any means, graphic, electronic, or mechanical, including photocopying,
recording, taping or by any information storage retrieval system
without the written permission of the author except in the case
of brief quotations embodied in critical articles and reviews.

Scripture taken from the HOLY BIBLE NEW INTERNATIONAL
VERSION. Copyright @ 1973, 1978, 1984 International Bible
Society. Used by permission of Zondervan Bible Publishers.

WestBow Press books may be ordered through
booksellers or by contacting:

WestBow Press
A Division of Thomas Nelson & Zondervan
1663 Liberty Drive
Bloomington, IN 47403
www.westbowpress.com
1 (866) 928-1240

Because of the dynamic nature of the Internet, any web addresses or
links contained in this book may have changed since publication and
may no longer be valid. The views expressed in this work are solely those
of the author and do not necessarily reflect the views of the publisher,
and the publisher hereby disclaims any responsibility for them.

Any people depicted in stock imagery provided by Thinkstock are
models,
and such images are being used for illustrative purposes only.
Certain stock imagery © Thinkstock.

ISBN: 978-1-5127-2512-4 (sc)

Library of Congress Control Number: 2015921222

Print information available on the last page.

WestBow Press rev. date: 1/14/2016

Dedicated to the awesome children God gave to me, Ben, Jennifer, Ken Doering and Collin Lytton, the wonderful loving people they married, Jenna and Abbe, and the angel grandbabies that will teach my children about God the Father in turn. Thanks to Tom Doering and Chuck Lytton, who I suspect will be great friends in heaven.

This book was written as series of short messages to members of a prayer group. A special thanks to all my fellow prayer group members for your dedication to prayer, your faith in Jesus Christ, and your encouragement and patience with me.

My family's newest teachers.

Why I must write

I write these stories about my children because I had to learn how far and how much my Father in heaven loves me. For you see, I was so broken a person from all the turmoil's of childhood that I really did not believe God could love me. It is as if I am compelled to write in order to do penance for every time I refused to acknowledge my Father's love.

I spent so many years trying to earn the love of my Heavenly Father having determined I was not loveable. I spent so many years begging him to love me I truly did not believe I deserved one ounce of His love. I was convinced that the bad things that happened to me were because I deserved them. I did the trade, shame and horror for guilt. With guilt I would reserve some sort of sense of control over my life. But since I was guilty, I judged myself using the harshest of measurements. No amount of penance ever seemed to cleanse me.

As a mother of four wonderful people, I learned that if I, who am imperfect, would risk my life to save my children, how much more did our Father God sacrifice in order to save me? I only have to look at Jesus on the cross for my answer. Why would I for even one minute believe my love for my children would be stronger than God's love for me? I did not think that outright, but I lived like it by not trusting God to hear my cry or not trusting God to be with me or not trusting God to come to my rescue.

Whenever I start to fall into the trap of self-pity or self-judgment, I have but to understand the lessons of love my children taught me.

"However, as it is written: No eye has seen, no ear has heard, no mind has conceived what God has prepared for those who love him." *(1 Corinthians 2:9)*

We cannot even fathom the incredible things God has waiting for us and I can imagine some pretty incredible things and even those will pale in comparison. And not for those whom He loves – He loves everyone, but for those who love him. If we will but open our hearts to him, He will open the flood gates of heaven's blessings to us.

And the offer has to be for everyone or God would not be God since to leave anyone out of the offer would mean his love would be less than his imperfect creation. Even more than I, who could never entertain the loss of anyone of my children for a single second, God who is perfect love cannot do anything less than love us beyond our measurements, beyond our wildest imaginations and beyond what eyes have seen and ears have ever heard.

Circle of Love

As I laid Collin down for bed one night, I remembered the bible verse, where Jesus told his disciples, "See that you do not look down on one of these little ones. For I tell you that their angels in heaven always see the face of my Father in heaven." *(Matthew 18:10)* By looking at the faces of each of the babies' angels, Father God knows instantly who is being loved and who is being mistreated. As I go to kiss my baby Collin's soft cheeks good-night, I think to myself, 'the Father in heaven will see the face of Collin's angel and a kiss of love will radiate from the angel's face to the Father's'. So I kissed his little cheeks twice, once for Collin and once more to beam a kiss of love directly to the Father.

This must be the circle of love I have heard about.

I looked for other circles in my life.

As I cleaned the floor at my mother's home, she asked, "Is it really bad?"

"No," I lie. Eyes that once watched me take my first steps across the floor can no longer see the spots which litter the surface of the room. Once she cared for me, now I care for her. It is the circle of life intertwined with love spiraling throughout the years. This is life's circle of obligations, which only death can end and only love can fulfill.

"I'll be done soon", I blurt, uncomfortable with the lie I just uttered. And so it was as the day came that I had to let go of my mother back to my Heavenly Father's loving arms.

We take turns expressing our love for one another at times giving to each other, at other times receiving. Each is the give and take of loving relationships and ultimately the result of the love showed to us by our Father in heaven. Love begets love as it circles our lives and embraces our hearts with no real beginning and no real end.

And the circle of love is complete.

"We love because he first loved us." *(1 John 4:19)*

Mother – Child Bonding

The first time I held him in my arms, I fell totally in love with my first born son, Ben. The minute of mother-child bonding was intense. I had heard about it. I had carried the baby within me for nine months. I knew when I conceived and knew it was a boy, but not until I held him, did I understand the extent of a mother's love. I knew then and there, it mattered not, a speeding car, a burning building, a mad-man with a gun, I would risk my life for my baby or die trying to protect this beautiful miracle in my arms. I rejoiced in his beauty. The big, soon-to-be-brown eyes and his beautiful face. It pleased me at how much he looked like his father. His tears would be my tears. His pains would be my pains. His disappointments would be my disappointments. We were tied by an invisible but iron clad cord of love. "Can a mother forget the baby at her breast and have no compassion on the child she has borne? Though she may forget, I will not forget you." *(Isaiah 49:15)*

How the weight of those words now touch me. "Forget my child," I ask? Not possible. So how could He possibly forget me? How many times have I started to pray as if He did not know what I needed or where I was emotionally? How many times have I asked, "Where are you God?" When my son cried out in the night, did I not run to his bed side? When he was ill, did I not nurse him back to health or incur a hurt that I did not try to kiss the pain away? You, Lord God, have stored all our tears in a bottle. Even the number of hairs on our head you have counted. You know the end of our days. You cover us like a mother hen covers her young with her wings. You wait as a mother with child longs for the day of the arrival. You even died for us, so that we might live. Like our birth, when we must have been afraid to leave the warmth of our mother's womb, our passing will be and yet, you Lord, will be there to hold us, look into our new born eyes and rejoice over us.

Ben

Fear Not

"Catch Me Mommy," cried my baby girl, Jennifer. All of five years of age, she stood at the edge of the pool wanting me to catch her just as I did her older brother. Little drops of water descended from her dark red curls as she held out her arms. So I said, "Go ahead and jump" and held out my arms toward her.

The depth of the pool where we both stood, was just slightly over her head and you could see that although she wanted to jump, she hesitated out of fear. I coaxed her as I knew, there was no way I would miss her. I could never miss her, I loved her too much. Yet she hesitated. Sizing up the situation, she leaned in closer to grasp my hands that I held out for her, thereby ensuring I would not miss. Finally she jumped and I caught her. The next time, I would not let her grasp my hands and stood just a little farther out. Each time she jumped she grew bolder having exercised her lessons in trust in me.

This is the way God teaches each of us. Each new lesson he stands back just a little farther to exercise our trust in Him. The first time He parted the waters for the Israelites, they stood on the bank of the Red Sea, trembling in fear of the approaching Egyptian Army. He provided a path through the depths and they moved past the waters on dry land. But the second time they crossed the waters it was different. 40 years later and going across the Jordan, the Israelites leading with the Ark of the Covenant would come to the bank of the Jordan River.

This time He waited until they stepped into the river before he parted the water for them to cross over. Each time it was a chance to trust Him. We hear the fear of economic issues. We see our saving dwindle or our jobs lost. Each day we are coaxed into a greater relationship of trust in Him. Trust Him and jump in the water. He will always catch you.

I remember the story of 12 men in a boat being tossed at sea when Jesus came walking to them on the water. "But Jesus said to them, 'Take courage! It is I. Do not be afraid.' 'Lord, if it is you,' Peter replied, 'tell me to come to you on the water.' 'Come,' he said. Then Peter got down out of the boat, walked on the water and came toward Jesus. But when he saw the wind, he was afraid and beginning to sink, cried out, 'Lord, save me.' Immediately Jesus reached out his hand and caught him." *(Matthew 14:27-31)*

"God is not a deceiver that He should offer to support us, and then, when we lean upon Him, should slip away from us." – St. Augustine.*

---

* *World of Quotes.* Copyright © 2013 <www.WorldofQuotes.com>.

Our Gifts to God

When Kenny came home from school one May afternoon, he was holding something behind his back. He also held all the expectation a six year old can hold, in his sparkling brown eyes as he pulled the gift wrapped in tissue paper and sealed with generous amounts of tape from behind his back. "Happy Mother's Day," he called as he handed me his treasure. I sat down and taking the precious gift in my hands, I unwrapped a hand-made necklace. I looked at the piece of baked clay with shiny sky blue glaze and attached to a long piece of dark purple yarn that he had made at school in anticipation of Mother's Day. "Oh, Kenny, it is beautiful," I cried and gave him the biggest mother hug I could give. "Kenny, I will treasure it forever," I promised and I meant it. That was years ago, but I remember it like it was yesterday. Even today those special Mother's Day gifts reside in my jewelry box alongside the necklaces of gold and silver, diamond rings and pearl earrings. In my heart, none of the jewelry means more to me than the Mother's Day Gifts. During Lent, it is a tradition to give some sacrifice to prepare our hearts for Easter Celebration. Like children making a Mother's Day gift, we carefully place our gifts before Jesus on Easter Sunday. And God, who has no need of our sacrifices or oblations, but wants hearts open to His call, carefully unwraps the gifts and places them in the jewelry box of His heart. Of what good can they be to an all knowing God? Only to the extent by which

we create them in love and offer them to Him as His
children. Though they are so insignificant in the presence
of His gifts to us, He cherishes them none the less.
I think I will work a little harder on my Lenten gift to
Jesus and I will wear my Mother's Day gifts - all of them
at once, to church on Mother's Day.

"The sacrifices of God are a broken spirit; a broken and
contrite heart, O God, you will not despise." *(Psalm 51:17)*

Are We There Yet?

I do not believe there is a parent alive who has taken their children on a car trip and not heard, "Are we there yet?" And it usually begins just as the trip is starting so you can guess it is going to be a very long journey. Their youth makes them impatient and their anticipation of what is to come accelerates their desire to be there. It will be useless to count the number of times they ask as eventually you will lose count. A journey of a thousand miles may begin with one step, but with kids it usually includes hundreds of, "are we there yet?"

Our life is such a journey. I have often asked God, "Why" but he does not answer that question. So now with every trial I ask, "Are we there yet?" He who began a good work in us will see it through to completion. Each encounter that we have to lean on God to get through is one more step in the journey. We can go forward with God leading the way or even carrying us, or lag behind and go backwards making our journey even longer. The good roads are fun and easy but the difficult paths seem to take forever. Sometimes the roads we are on take us with others we were meant to love and help along. Sometimes our paths cross with those who are broken and needing mercy and forgiveness. Sometimes we are the ones needing mercy and forgiveness. When I am tempted to ask, "Why did we go this way?" I am reminded that Jesus is the way and I am secure again. When I wonder, "Why did these things happen," I am reminded that Jesus is the truth and I am grounded again. When I question if I can continue, I am reminded that Jesus is the life and until I am with him in heaven, I am still on the right path.

Since I got up this morning and am writing this, it means that I am not there yet. I will check again with God tomorrow morning by saying, "Good Morning Jesus, Are we there yet?"

"Thomas said to him, 'Lord, we do not know where you are going, so how can we know the way?' Jesus answered, 'I am the Way, and the Truth, and the Life. No one comes to the Father except through me.'" *(John 14:5-6)*

Beginning to rise again

After my husband, Tom, died, I moved with my children 1,000 miles back home to St. Louis. The entire process was overwhelming and settling into a new home chaotic to say the least. Ben who just turned six and Jennifer who turned four never got along and then it seemed as if they were worse than ever. Caring for the three of them, moving and grieving seemed more than I could handle.

I sat the two older babies down. Time for a talk. "Look, I know things are hectic right now, but we need to pull it together. This fighting has to stop. If we cannot get it together, this family might have to split up because I do not know how much I can take," I explained to them. The result of the first talk ended in failure. I tried again a week later. The result was worse than before. Their fighting increased all the more. "What am I going to do, God," I cried.

I put them down for their naps and cuddled the baby. The words of the gospel seemed to cry back out to me, "Do not be afraid." I realized that reasoning with the babies had only frightened them all the more. We were all afraid. Terrible big changes had just taken place and no one, not even their Mom was sure things could work out. It is just that they showed their fear by acting out. How could I undo my terrible mistake? "I totally messed up, God," I prayed. "What do I do now?"

I do believe the Holy Spirit gave me the ideas I needed to start the healing. I could encourage Ben and that would be easy. Jennifer on the other hand, even at four was way too bright for a complete reversal. I would have to do something else for her. Do not talk to them, talk to baby Kenny as they play was the thought placed in my heart.

When they got up from their naps, I brought Kenny down stairs and changed his diaper near them as they played. "Kenny," I started watching the others out of the corner of my eye, "no one is going to break up this family. We are strong and we are going to make it together. No one and nothing is going to separate us!" I declared.

Immediately Ben came over and taking Kenny's head in his hands looking down into his sweet face, said, "That's right Kenny, no one is going to break up this family." My little red headed girl Jennifer, just looked at us suspiciously. But she paid attention. I wish I could say that ended the fighting but it seemed to help all of us. It was as if we hit a small turning point. We were no longer careening off the cliff of grief but slowly making our way back out of a very deep, black canyon.

"When they came to the home of the synagogue ruler, Jesus saw a commotion, with the people crying and wailing loudly. He went in and said to them, 'Why all this commotion and wailing? The child is not dead but asleep.' But they laughed at him. After he put them all out, he took the child's father and mother and the disciples who were there with him, and went in where the child was. He took her by the hand and said to her, 'Talitha koumi,' which means, "Little girl, I say to you get up.' Immediately the girl stood up and walked around." *(Mark 5:38-42)*

I Don't want to be that 'Holy'

There were times my children would complain, "Why do we have to go to church?" I would tell them that it was God's job to make us holy so we had to present ourselves to him so He could work on us. That is when they would tell me in so many words, "We don't want to be that holy". They did not understand that we were made in God's image to love, adore and serve him and in doing so, we find the true meaning for our existence. We find contentment in who we truly are. I was irritated with their attitude until I realized that I draw the line on holiness myself. How often might I say, "I went to church today, so I am done for the week?" Or argue with God that "I already gave to that cause." Even though we know we were called to be the salt of the earth and the light on the hill, it would be rare for us to go all the way to that invisible line of *enough* versus *not enough* in our service to the Almighty. It is not rare for us to compare ourselves to others to see if we have done just that little bit more than they have done. This might make us, 'holier than thou,' but not necessarily faithful servants. Do we not worry, that God just might ask too much of us or ask more than we really want to give? So if today we hear his voice, we might just say, "No Lord, I am finished being holy for the day."

Just how "holy" is too "holy" anyway or is it even possible? I think it takes a lot of honest soul searching to really know if we are doing enough to serve the Lord our God, or love him with all of our hearts and all of our souls and all of our minds. We just might see the empty areas in our lives which He wants to fill. I mean, really, after all, we do not want to be those 'saints' who are forever looking up at heaven and beating our chests do we? Or those who pray all day long? Or those who are always doing something for someone? Or those who are taking that time to attend a bible study or the prayer group. Are not some people too 'Heavenly minded' to be any earthly good?

I do not know what the answer to these questions are myself. I am guessing it is a life long journey which is measured in love. God's work in me is never done. Maybe when I close my eyes for the last time I will know the full meaning of holy.

"Do you not know you are the temple of God and that the spirit of God dwells in you? If anyone destroys God's Temple, God will destroy that person; for the temple of God, which you are, is holy." *(1 Corinthians 3: 16-17)*

"My God, I want to do what you want. Your teachings are in my heart." *(Psalm 40:8)*

Catch Us if You Can

When my oldest children were still quite young, I made it a point of trying to always kiss them good bye as they ran out of the house and down the street to the school bus. My contrary children made it into a game to see if they could avoid the hug and kiss and would race out the door just ahead of me. Luckily, I was quicker and faster than them for the most part and was just able to catch them. I would kiss my hand and tag them in passing with the good bye kiss. We all delighted in the game so much that even the neighbor boy would join in the game of chase.

 I do not know if they understood how important it was to me then to give them that kiss. A few years earlier, as we were saying good bye to their father as he rode his bike down the street to work, I had a small still voice speak in my heart telling me to make sure I always kissed him good bye. Then a week later, we would all kiss him good bye for the last time. The morning he died, I was not up as usual as he got ready to go because the baby had been fussy through the night and the children were all still sound asleep. I will always regret not getting up with him that morning.

 Death has a way of putting things into perspective. We do not know the hour or the day. But neither do we know the hour or the day of Christ's Second coming, when the final enemy, death, is destroyed once and for all. Death may be sad, but how much greater will the joy of reuniting with loved ones be? Christ is already the victor.

Mary Lytton

We will rise again with Him and He will wipe every tear away. Our hope is truly in the Resurrection.

You can run if you want, but our Lord is quicker and will tag you with a kiss today.

"The last enemy to be destroyed is death." *(1 Corinthians 15:26)*

Babies at Rest

I was always amazed at how quickly my frustration with the children would disappear when I would check on them as they slept. Looking at their sweet sleeping angelic faces renewed in my heart all that was wonderful about being their mother. No tears to dry or fights to settle, I could gaze on their beautiful innocent cheeks and heads. Somehow as they slept, peace seemed to descend from heaven.

The Lord calls us to enter into His rest. Is this like the state of sleeping babies? Those who are so totally dependent on us that they can sleep with an innocent peace comforted in knowing mom is just a cry away? Like a weaned child we are held in His arms and are called to be innocent babes, believing and trusting in His love for us.

When did we forget this? At some point, we quit trusting in His love for us and somehow started to believe that everything was in our hands. At some time in our life, we quit trusting Him to watch over us. This is why we must be born again. Go back to the innocent, trusting children our Father created us to be. If it were not so, Jesus would not have said it was. When they fought over who was the greatest, Jesus brought the child into their mist. When they tried to keep the children away, Jesus said, "'Let them come to me."

Help us, Oh Lord, to be those trusting loving children we once were.

Mary Lytton

"Cast your cares upon the Lord, and he will sustain you."
(Psalm 55:22)

"I will lie down and sleep in peace, for you alone O Lord,
make me dwell in safety." *(Psalm 4:8)*

I hear you Cry

They say that a mother or a father will tune into the voice of their child. I know this to be true. When Jennifer was a baby, I had just put her to bed in her crib and fell fast asleep myself, when I was awakened by her cry. She was beyond the point of needing to get up in the middle of the night, so I was very surprised to hear her cry so soon after being put to bed for the night. I got up, picked her up and sat on the bed in order to rock her back to sleep. I knew instinctively that her cry was not of pain or hunger but it wasn't until I sat down on the bed that I was awake enough to realize there was a very loud police siren blaring just outside our bedroom windows. Even though the siren was a least ten times louder than my baby girl's cry, it was not the siren that I awoke to, it was Jennifer's cry. The siren had startled her. She cried out in fear and it awoke me.

If I, an imperfect mother can hear my child's cry, then how much more our heavenly Father must listen for our cries. Just as I wanted to sooth my child's fears, He too must wish to hold us in his arms and rock us in his embrace. Even now my adult daughter's cries tug at my heart. She could never grow so old that my heart would not break when her heart breaks. We are so precious to him, that He saves every tear we shed and longs to wipe them from our eyes. Her pains are my pains. She is so tied to my heart that she could not suffer without my suffering with her. So too, He must hurt when we hurt. After all we are created in His image.

Once in my anger, I yelled at my heavenly Father, "I was just a child, how could you let these terrible things happen to me?" I can honestly tell you, that God in heaven never answers the question "Why," lest He set himself up for our judgment and with our limited understanding we would judge Him unfairly. The only answer I could come to was, "I knew you would need a savior, 2,000 years before you were even born, and I sent my son to die for you so that you could live in spite of every terrible thing that could or would happen." And He was there with me, I just did not trust him enough to believe it. It is only when I looked back that I saw more than his foot prints on the beach, but also the marks of the cross dragging in the sand behind us. He carried us both.

So once again, I come before the throne of Christ, humble and needing to trust that when I cry, He hears and answers me.

"I cried out to my God for help. From his temple he heard my voice; my cry came before him, into his ears." *(Psalm 18:6)*

Jennifer

Disappointment

Ben was in Cub Scouts and once a year they have a soap box derby with the little cars that they put together with their dad's (or in this case, their mother's) help. It was obvious from the beginning that with my help, Ben did not stand a chance. I did not know anything about these cars, how to put them together and how to make them run. Ben really wanted to win, too. We returned home in defeat. "You did a good job even if you did not win," I told him. We could try again next year. We would do much better. After all, hadn't we had much worse losses in our life? All of my pep talks seemed hollow. Still, disappointment is a fact of life and no matter how hard I try, I cannot protect my little ones from it. Nor should I. How would they ever grow up to be mature adults if I protected them from all of life's disappointments? How would they ever become feeling people if they never experienced being let down and not getting everything they wanted? How much more would 'winning' mean to him after knowing loss? As much as I wanted to protect him from losing, I knew he had to learn how to do it. I would hurt with him and experience his pain because I knew all about disappointment and pain and my love for him would not allow me to be insulated from his feelings. In spite of everything, he still had a choice, to try again or quit. The race is really a test of what we are truly made of when we do not win.

So, how much more when we are disappointed in life, must God our Father ache with us. He wants us to win, but sometimes winning the race is not the true victory. The victory is more in passing the test after failing. We tell our children that it is not if we win or lose, it is how we play the game. Meanwhile, we put up the trophies as if they were true signs of greatness when the real trophies are the races we ran where we did not win but we also did not quit. They are the races we lost in terms of not finishing first but continued the race in face of great obstacles, or competitions where we did not steal, cheat or lie and could lose with grace and good nature toward those who did win. These are the real tests to pass. Greatness sometimes comes in the midst of our greatest defeats when we look to God instead of what we may have lost and treat others around us with love. How awful it is to both lose the race and fail the test afterwards.

St. Paul talked about running the race, but not winning it. He never said that God would only be pleased if we won. Instead, God, as our cheerleader and proud Father, waits at the finish line and no matter where we placed in the race, He is there to say, "Well done, good and faithful servant".

"I have fought the good fight. I have finished the race. I have kept the faith." *(2 Timothy 4:7)*

I am Running Away

Jennifer was my fiery spirited red headed baby girl. She was also my only child on whom reverse psychology worked. If I said, "Stay," she would go and if I said, "Go," she would stay. So the day she proclaimed, with all the determination of a seven-year-old going on 17 could muster, that she was running away from home, I was faced with a terrible dilemma. If I said, "No, you cannot go" which is what my mother's heart longed to cry out, she might be all the more determined to leave. If I said, "Go ahead and leave," even if I knew it was to use reverse psychology, I feared the scars it might leave on her heart as well as my own. So I stopped in my tracks and blurted out, "OK, if you must". But then I added, "I have to get my camera so I can take a picture of you leaving." I hoped that would stall for time to keep her from going. I feared with all my heart that she might actually follow through with her threat but issuing a command to stay would only have fueled her desire to leave. With her brothers laughing and enjoying her embarrassment as we took her picture, she relented and came back inside the house.

In my heart, I knew this was pay back for my own youth.

As a teenager, I had come to a point in my life that my only hope in living was to run away. I packed my bag and went to the door. There was no one who would stop me, I thought. But my Father in heaven had other plans for me. He let forth a storm of driving rain so hard that all I could do was stand under the porch and watch with dismay. I would be drenched before even leaving the driveway much less the highway. He let it rain until I finally gave up. I have no doubt that if He had not done so, I would have become one of the statistics on runaways.

There are times in our life where we ask, "Where are you God?" It seems as if we only see his hand after the fact, in the middle of the storm holding us and caring for us. How many times did He have to tell us to "Fear Not?" We can never run away from his love. If we go to the highest heaven, He is there. If we go down to farthest depths, He is there too. We can run but never be more than a call away, ever so near to us is He. His words never tell us anything different. It is our lack of trust that keeps us from seeing His hands in our life. 'My sheep know my voice', and the Father knows the cry of his children.

"Where can I go from your Spirit? Where can I flee from your presence? If I go up to the heavens, you are there; if I make my bed in the depths, you are there. If I rise on the wings of the dawn, if I settle on the far side of the sea; even there your hand will guide me, your right hand hold me fast." *(Psalm 139: 7-10)*

See Yourself as God Sees You

My son, Kenny was my sweet, compliant one. He is a talented, loving, intelligent, thoughtful person. I could go on and on about him. And yes, I love all of my children and I do not have favorites. I just recognize that Kenny had many wonderful traits. But my son went through a period in his adolescence where he became very depressed and lost hope in life. I was filled with anxiety, fear and sadness for him. I prayed that he would not give up entirely. I knew that he did not see just how wonderful he truly was. He was afraid to let himself shine and the rejection from peers kept him from showing his true self. In so many ways he was following in my footsteps of adolescent depression and fears. I would meet him at the door when he came home from work to talk to him. I would seek out others to aid in my quest to help him find himself. I had his older brother and sister call him to talk to him and give him hope. No matter what, I was not willing to give up on him. I would never give up in helping him see who he truly was.

I can see now my Father's hand in my adolescence and know that I was foremost in his mind as He did everything he could to bring hope back to my heart. No matter what, He was not willing to give up on me. It is the hand of evil that tries to tell us how horrible, ugly, hopeless, unlovable or stupid we are. These are the lies of Satan. God has never created junk. Each one of us is wonderful, beautiful and unique in His eyes and He looks at us with the greatest of love even more than we would do looking at our own babies in our arms.

We need to ask the Father to let us see ourselves as He sees us. When we truly see who we are in Christ, we see the true beauty God created.

No matter where you are right now. No matter where you have been. Father God is waiting with open arms and a loving spirit to pick you up in his arms and look at you and smile. You are his child.

"I praise you because I am fearfully and wonderfully made; your works are wonderful, I know that full well." *(Psalm 139:14)*

Let Me Kiss Your Tears Away

Collin was not like my other children when he got hurt. My other children would come to me for hugs and kisses. "Let Mommy kiss the hurt to make it better," I would tell them. Like some magic potion, kisses healed the boo-boo and hugs took the pain away. They believed it and I prayed it would work. Every hurt and pain they received hurt me too. I suffered with them. I hurt for them. I worried when the hurts and pains were too big for kisses and hugs. I cried when the pains were too deep for both of us and when they grew too big to let me rock them in my arms.

But Collin was different. Even when so very little, when he got hurt he would run into his room, close the door and hide under the covers. If the hurt was very bad, he would hide under the bed. Coaxing him out took lots of time and almost hurt me more because he would not let me console him. It hurt me to think, he did not know how much I longed to hug the tears away. "Just let me be your Mommy," I thought to myself. It did not matter to me if the hurt was from his own childish doings.

We cannot love our children more than God loves us. We cannot long to wipe the tears away more than He does. We cannot hurt more for their suffering than He does. I did not know that. When young in faith, I always ran away from Him afraid my pain was my own fault for which He would say, "See, I told you not to do that" or "Serves you right." I was so terribly wrong. I did not understand how much He loved me. I hid under the covers crying my heart out not realizing how much He wanted to comfort me. It took Collin to teach me that when I hurt, I should run to the loving arms of my Heavenly Father so He can kiss the hurts away.

"The Lord is close to the broken hearted and saves those who are crushed in Spirit." *(Psalm 34:18)*

Your Biggest Fan

When Ben would play basketball, I would watch his games sitting on the bleachers with the rest of the parents. I confess to getting a bit carried away with cheering him on. Once when there were only a few parents present, apparently I was rather loud and later my son asked me to not cheer so much. I guess I embarrassed him. But I could not help myself. I was his biggest fan and seeing him succeed was near and dear to my heart. I loved to brag when he made a shot or did well at blocking a shot. I always congratulated him on a game well played even when he did not win. It was good enough that he finished · the game.

This is exactly what God wants for us. He is our biggest cheerleader, encouraging us on and singing our praises. He is not keeping score about how many times we missed the ball or made the shot. He wants us to run the good race and fight the good fight. In his book *The Applause of Heaven*, Max Lucado tells us that when we finish our time on earth, our loved ones and Jesus will be there at the finish line cheering us on and welcoming us home again. They wait for us like expectant parents awaiting the birth of their babies, with longing excitement.

Ken and Abbe's wedding with Jenna,
Ben, Chuck, Mary and Jennifer

Trust Him, He is taking care of you

It was a terrible prank call. Why someone should want to call a widow with three small children and tell her they saw a prowler around her house, is beyond me. But I did what I could to protect my children. I became Mother bear. I called the police and told them what the person said and then I told the children as calmly as possible to get in the car, we were going for a ride. I did not want to scare them so I did not explain why we would go for a ride, I just said, "Let's do this and maybe we can have some fun." They questioned me why I would do such a thing, but I could not give them the answer. Luckily the police arrived very quickly and could find no evidence any prowler was anywhere around. They determined the call was prank and since the person calling had only given me a first name and I was too shaken to ask for a last name, they could not determine who the call came from. (This was before Caller ID) We never left the house and once the police came, there was no need to leave. I would have fought to the death for my children. But even more, I did not want them to lose their peace and be afraid. Just as I would have physically protected them, I wanted to protect their gentle spirits from useless anxiety and fear, since I was still in control.

When I look back, there were many times when for some reason, I had to change my plans because something came up at the last moment. Once it was missing car keys that delayed my trip. Once it was lost shoes. Only later did it became clear that the change in plans was from God protecting me. But most of the time, I never knew the reason why. I truly believe there is no such thing as a coincidence. Everything works according to God's plan for those He has chosen and called to be his own. How much more must God work to protect us from useless anxiety and fears? If only we would become like his little children and not ask why, just get in the car and go for a ride and trust him to take us where we need to go.

"Where to, Lord?"

"There is no fear in love. But, perfect love drives out fear, because fear has to do with punishment. The one who fears is not made perfect in love." *(1 John 4:18)*

Not an Accident

When I got pregnant with Collin, it was a surprise. My youngest child, Kenny at that time was ten years old and I had given all the baby things away thinking there would be no more babies. People were as surprised as I was, I think. When I said I was pregnant, they asked, "Is it (he) an accident?" I may not have planned his coming nor did I expect him but how could any of our little ones be accidents? I know, in a perfect world every pregnancy would be longed for, prayed about and anticipated with great joy. But many times in our real world, they just happen and a lot of times when we least expect it. I laughed when I told my husband, Chuck, I was pregnant and he said, "How did this happen?" In my heart of hearts, Collin was not an accident nor was he mass-produced or an evolutionary by-product. Collin was lovingly designed by the Master Creator of us all and placed into a home where he could teach us as much as we could teach him. He was designed by love to love us and be loved by us. Every ounce of his being was deliberately knitted within my womb and set into place by the hand of the loving Father who knew exactly what was needed. Not a single cell in his body was an accident or a product of merely a physical world in motion and change.

The God of the Universe who spun all the stars in the sky and designed all the galaxies and yet is mindful of every tear that we cry and has given each of us a special name does not create accidents or create by accident. He knits us together creating our inmost beings in the secret recesses of our mother's womb. He creates us out of love to be loved and to love in return. In our materialistic world that gives man the impression he can save himself with enough money or strength or intelligence or even with dooms day prepping, Father God has already designed us with everything we need and has already provided salvation. What a great reason to rejoice and be glad for you are lovingly and fearfully and wonderfully made!

"For you created my inmost being; you knit me together in my mother's womb. I praise you because I am fearfully and wonderfully made; your works are wonderful" *(Psalm 139:13)*

Collin, Chuck and Ken at the beach.

Imitation of the Father

Jennifer was almost six years old, when I started to toilet-train her younger brother, Kenny. I got out the potty chair from storage and placed it in the bathroom. Then as I coaxed Ken into the bathroom, Jennifer would take over the job as if she were the mommy. It lifted my heart in joy to see her imitate me in such a loving motherly way as she took him a little book to look at while sitting there or brought him a drink in a Sippy cup. I remember her little voice giving him encouragement and praise and just had to smile. I had no doubts that someday she would be a loving mother to her own children.

They say "imitation is the sincerest form of flattery." But I think that when we look to Christ and imitate him in his love for our brothers and sisters, our imitation becomes the sincerest form of worship. More than just words are our deeds and deeds done in imitation of Christ must fill the Father's heart with joy. See if today, you can find a way to imitate Christ's unquenchable love for others just to fill the Father's heart with joy!

"Dear friend, do not imitate what is evil but what is good. Anyone who does what is good is from God." *(3 John 1:11)*

Ken

Stories with a Promise

Some of my most favorite times spent with my children were when they would curl up next to me on the couch or bed as I read them a story or two or three. They never seemed to get tired of my reading to them and would ask for more and more until I was too tired to read another word. It did not matter if they heard the story a dozen times or more. And they loved it when I would interact with them as we huffed and puffed and tried to blow the house down or if we used funny voices for the characters. It seemed to bring a special light to their lives if only for the special time we spent together enjoying each other's company. One story of a train that could, bringing forth the story of a mother with her children reading together ever bonding in love that promised to last forever.

So, it doesn't surprise me that Jesus would sit and tell the people stories about his Father's Kingdom, stories that to us do not always make a lot of sense. Like the story of when the shepherd leaves the 99 to find the one lost sheep or when the woman who lost the coin tears up the house looking for it then has to proclaim it to all the neighbors. He told them stories with promises to explain the truth to a people in darkness to bring light and hope into their lives. Promises of hope, to be with them till the end. Promises to be present if two or more are gathered together in His name. Promises to search for them if they were lost. Stories that created testimony of his love in their life. Testimony that continues the promises and gives birth to others' testimonies. Never be afraid to tell your story especially to those in darkness who need to hear of the wonderful things God has done in your life. Never tire of telling it or of thanking God for it. Even if you have to huff and puff or use funny sounding voices to tell it. It has to be told to help create new stories with a promise.

"They overcame him by the blood of the Lamb, and by the word of their testimony; they did not love their lives so much as to shrink from death." *(Revelation 12:11)*

"So Paul and Barnabas spent considerable time there, speaking boldly for the Lord, who confirmed the message of his grace by enabling them to do miraculous signs and wonders." *(Acts 14:3)*

I will ask for you

My children were pretty bright in knowing how to get things they really wanted. They would get together and decide on something – usually something like getting me to take them to Chucky Cheese or some sort of thing like that and they knew that it was harder for me to turn down two or all three of them at the same time. They approached it as if it was a cause. They also knew that it might be easier for me to agree if the baby Kenny asked for them. It was not that Kenny was better or cuter or more loved. They just knew that the baby held slightly more sway with mom. Not sure why they thought this, but I always knew why Ken was asking for things that he really did not have a true desire for. He was asking for their benefit because he loved them. I was on to them but they were correct. I found it difficult to look into the eyes of all three of them at the same time and tell them no. When I hesitated and it looked like they might not get what they were asking for, they would plead all the more. Time, money and energy, considered, they could count on it happening – within reason of course. It delighted me to grant their requests and sort of amused me how they came together on a project. They had faith that I loved them and they could come and ask. They had intelligence to know how to ask, en masse with pleading eyes and hearts. And they knew I loved them and had a hard time turning them down. And they certainly were persistent! Are we not to be the same, "like children," in approaching our Lord?

So, when I reflect on our Lord's words, when He spoke about trying to convince your brother of something and if you cannot do so, to go get others to come with you, well, I see my children at work. Like my children, I know I can come boldly before the throne of God and He will grant, within great wisdom, that which is right and best for me. How much more He must delight in giving us the desires of our heart? How He must be pleased when his children come before his throne in one accord. We should never tire of praying for each other, keeping persistent in our requests and knowing that together our prayers are magnified.

"In a certain town there was a judge who neither feared God nor cared about men. And there was a widow in that town who kept coming to him with the plea, 'Grant me justice against my adversary.' For some time he refused. But finally he said to himself, 'Even though I do not fear God, nor care about men, yet because this widow keeps bothering me, I will see that she gets justice, so that she will not eventually wear me out with her coming.'" *(Luke 18:2-5)*

There is always a plan

God always has a plan. He is not required to check with us first. Nor is He open to our opinions. That is because He has the Big Plan. It is the one we cannot see. It is the one He created from the beginning of eternity and will see it through. A lot of times we ask "Why God?" and there is silence. If we hear that still small voice, He might tell us, "Trust me, I have a plan."

When Collin was born, I was 40 years old and I knew another child would not be possible. I thought of how the only flesh and blood child my second husband would have, had Down's Syndrome. I could not understand God's plan for me. Even now, I sit and wonder at the plan.

My father was elderly and in poor health when Collin was born. He called me in tears and asked, "Is it my fault this happened?" He had lived a very hard life. Nearly starving to death as a child in the depression, he at six years of age was working two jobs, paper route before school and delivering groceries after school, just so his mother would have money to feed the younger children. Then drafted into WWII, he saw the worst that mankind can do to each other by surviving the Battle of the Bulge and then helping to free the concentration camp, Bergen-Belsen. He was quite a scrapper. He learned how to survive and sometimes did things that later he was ashamed of. "Is it my fault?" His question took me by surprise.

I remembered the story of the man born blind from birth. "Tell us Rabbi," they asked, "Whose fault was it, his mother's or his father's?" Jesus told them, it was neither. The man was born blind so that the glory of God could be manifested. I am so grateful for a God who reassures us that when things happen that seem to make no sense at all, that we do not have to live in guilt as if bad things happen only to bad people. We cannot see the plan He has for us. He is still Father God. He is still in control. He does not punish us for every offense but offers continual forgiveness. How very fortunate we are to be loved by so great a God!

Manifest in us, Lord, your glory, that your plan for us may be fulfilled!

"'For I know the plans I have for you,' declares the Lord, 'plans to prosper you and not harm you, plans to give you hope and a future.'" *(Jeremiah 29:11)*

"You Don't Love Me"

Collin was angry with me when he uttered those words, "You don't love me." But he knew better and was only saying that to try to manipulate me into giving him what he wanted. He was trying that angle where he hoped I would work at proving him wrong. I called his bluff and Collin is not able to play poker, he knew I had him dead to rights. He knew I loved him. He knows I love him very well. I do not have to prove it, I show it to him all the time in hundreds of ways. There are too many for a mother to count. The thought would never enter my mind, "Say, I think I have shown my love too many times today, I think I will stop for a while." Seriously? When does love ever take a break? The desires of my heart keep my loved ones ever present in my mind and heart.

How often I complained to God that He did not love me. I really thought that it was possible that God might not care. Could we possibly ever count the ways He loves us?

All who take delight in Him, He will grant the desires of their hearts. [Psalm 37:4] He is our shepherd and we lack nothing. [Psalm 23:1]. We can take shelter in the shadow of his almighty presence[Psalm 91:1] He will fill us with joy in His Presence and eternal pleasures at his right hand. [Psalm 16:11] He will counsel us with his loving eye on us. [Psalm 32:8]. As the heavens tower over the earth, so God's love towers over the faithful. [Psalm 103:11] He will renew our strength so we can soar on wings like eagles, run and not get tired and walk and not grow faint. [Isaiah 40:31] He will heal the brokenhearted, proclaim freedom for captives and release prisoners from darkness. [Isaiah 61:1]. Even while we were still in sin, He sent his only begotten son to die for us.

No, it is not possible to count all the ways. His love is eternal. But we have an eternity to continue counting.

Out of the Mouths of Babies, Comes Words of Wisdom and Perfect Praise.

I was out of breath by the time Collin and I found our seats at Church Sunday morning. Late again and trying to come in quietly was not an option with Collin who insists on shaking everyone's hands as he comes in. And when he saw Father Blessing and Joe Witkowski up at the altar he waved as big as possible to say 'Hello.' To make it worse, Father Ed Griesedieck was coming down the aisle right at us. No one missed us coming in late. Missing shoes, stubborn Collin issues, slow vehicles in front of me, you name it, it slowed us down. It seems to be that way almost every Sunday morning. I was worried about what people thought about us coming in late again. That's when I heard the kissing noises. Collin had picked up the missal and saw that Jesus's picture was on the front cover. He began to kiss the picture in earnest. Like a pin to a balloon, my inner spirit sank. While I was upset about being late, Collin saw the bigger picture. He found Jesus and covered him with kisses. While I thought of my image among others, he only cared about saying hello to Jesus.

How many times that little rascal has humbled me. How many times, just when I am at my wit's end, he has shown me up. When they told me after his birth, special children teach us so much, I thought it was just a platitude meant to cheer me up with little to no truth. I was so wrong. He teaches me every day. Jesus, here's a kiss for you today. And every time I kiss Collin's face, may we both know, I kiss you, too.

"Then he turned toward the woman and said to Simon, 'Do you see this woman? I came into your house. You did not give me any water for my feet, but she wet my feet with her tears and wiped them with her hair. You did not give me a kiss, but this woman, from the time I entered, has not stopped kissing my feet. You did not put oil on my head, but she has poured perfume on my feet. Therefore, I tell you, her many sins have been forgiven-for she loved much. But he who has been forgiven little, loves little.'" *(Luke 7:44 -47)*

"From the lips of children and infants, you have ordained praise." *(Psalm 8:2)*

Collin with mentor and friend, Joe Witkowski.

Too Busy

When my older children were little, mornings before school were hectic. I would rouse them, get them dressed for school, make breakfast and lunches if necessary and a hundred things that mothers and fathers around the world do for children every day.

I do not know of many mothers or fathers that are not overworked and constantly in demand. So one morning when Ken was still little, I was fixing breakfast for Ben and Jennifer before they left for school, when he came up to me and tugged on my pant leg. It just happened that I was trying to cook them a nice breakfast for test week, so eggs, bacon and pancakes were simultaneously cooking and as I was trying to juggle it all, I said to Ken, "Just a minute." A minute to Kenny was approximately two seconds and he tugged on my pant leg again. "Just a minute, honey," I said again. And another two seconds passed and he tugged a third time. With everything spattering on the stove, I turned to him saying, "WHAT? WHAT? WHAT!"

He took a deep breath and said in very disappointed voice, "Good Morning, Mommy."

You know what it is like when you just realized you blew it big time with someone, especially an angel of a person? I was humbled again.

I turned off the stove and gathered him into my arms. "I am so sorry, Kenny, I was just busy," I cried.

"Mommy, I only wanted to tell you, good morning," he said looking up at me with those beautiful brown eyes.

And what a beautiful morning it was holding him in my arms.

How many mornings has our Lord tried to get our attention to tell us "Good Morning?" No wonder the psalms tell us that the Lord will wake us with his presence. How else will he ever get our attention once we are up and running for the day?

I am probably the worst of the worst, in that I am action driven. Given a set of tasks, I will go until they are completed or until I realize I cannot finish them. Making time for God is somewhere either before I start running or after I can run no more. Taking time out, just seems to go against my grain. Our God is a jealous God who wants us for himself. He wants to be part of our lives, not just a piece in the morning and a piece at night before bed. He wants to live in us and with us. He wants to wake us with a hug and kiss and say, "Good Morning."

Do you have a minute for him to tell you how much He loves you today? Stop what you are doing just for a minute to tell him, "Good Morning."

"Arise, shine, for your light has come, and the glory of the Lord rises upon you." *(Isaiah 60:1)*

Collin's Song

His little song could hardly be heard above the sounds of the surf on the beach, the other children at play and the sea gulls over-head. Collin was building a sand castle and singing to his heart's delight, 'No School today' to a song whose melody only he could really hear. A tear of joy came to my eyes hearing it and thinking, 'Little rascal, he is really happy.' On some days he must be greatly encouraged to even smile, like when he is getting on the school bus in the morning. On other days, like that day, his joy flowed as freely out of his heart as the surf on to the beach.

After years of living through depression, sometimes I can be heard singing a song, too. After He lifted me out of the mud, put my feet on high sturdy ground and a new song in my heart. Our Lord, our God longs to see us singing to our heart's delight a song of victory of joy over sorrow, love over hate and life over death. Shout with joy for your salvation is at hand and give glad tiding to the day. For this is the day the Lord has made let us be joyful and glad. It is our joy that tells the world we are different, and our love for each other that tells the world we have been set apart for a special purpose. When the world sees us, it should see the light on the hill and taste the salt of the earth. Sing, your Lord is singing with you.

"You turned my wailing into dancing for me. You removed my sackcloth and clothed me with joy, that my heart may sing to you and not be silent." *(Psalm 30:11-12)*

Who You Are and Who You Are With

I was recently talking with two friends about our children and about our own upbringing. One friend told me that her mother always said to her before she went out with friends, "Remember who you are and remember who you represent." My other friend responded with her grandmother's saying, "Tell me who you are with and I will tell you who you are." When I look back at my children growing up and remember their friends, I smile since they had good friends to associate with and were usually good role models. When Ben was in his last years of high school, before everyone had laptops, his friends would arrive at sunset with their desktop computers, monitors and keyboards, set up all their computers downstairs, hook them up together and play war games against each other all night long. Then in the morning as politely as they came in, they would take all their stuff and go home to sleep most of the day away. We knew where they were and what they were doing. They were assembled in my home to spend time in friendship and unity. I knew who they were and what they represented and in a few short years they would all separate and go on their own ways. I was pleased because I was well aware of all the other things they could be doing and chose not to do. They had formed a tight and cohesive bond of friendship to ward off the intense pressure from peers not so well grounded. It gave them the strength to not conform to the world but to be their selves. It gave them the ability to be in the world of teens but not be like so many who were lost and seeking their self-esteem in activities destined to destroy them.

Christ called us his friend that we would be grounded in Him and not conform to the world but be strengthened to show Christ's light to the world. That is why we need to seek out fellow members of Christ's body to spend time in friendship and unity. When our Father in heaven looks at us He can smile because He knows that when we are together we represent His beloved Son, shining the light of Christ from within us to all the world.

"A faithful friend is a strong defense; and he that hath found him, hath found a treasure. Nothing can be compared to a faithful friend, and no weight of gold and silver is able to countervail the goodness of his fidelity. A faithful friend is the medicine of life and immortality; and they that fear the Lord shall find him. He that feareth God, shall likewise have good friendship: because according to him shall his friend be." *(Sirach 6:14-17)*

Safely Home Again

As a very small child, Collin did not have an ounce of fear in his bones but not because he was truly courageous. He never understood what dangers the world could present. So at every chance, he would escape the house and look for adventure. After a long search, he would be brought back home by his weary and emotionally exhausted parents and siblings. It was a common occurrence for me to run into the house and call to all of Collin's family, "Collin has escaped again!" With that rally cry, everyone would jump up and take off in different directions to hunt Collin down and bring him home. Once or twice the police were called, when it seemed that he had really disappeared this time. Neighbors often joined in the search. We would have searched the earth for that little rascal even though it was his own fault when he got lost. We never once said, "Well, that's too bad. Hope he makes it home OK." We never thought, "Let's wait awhile and see what happens." When Collin was found unhurt, we would cry for relief that he was found safe and sound. We never said, "Go away you little trouble maker." Instead we covered him with hugs and kisses.

How much more does God the father love us? How much more, when we stray does he cry out to the angels, "Well, he (or she) has escaped, again." And all the angels take flight to find us. Do we sometimes think that when we stray, God may not want to see us again? Do we approach our Father like a dog with his tail between his legs hoping he will not punish us? Or that when we get hurt in our wayward adventures that God may think, "Serves them right going off like that." We often see the Father as we ourselves were fathered on earth.

But Jesus told us different. The prodigal son returned to the father amidst hugs and tears and kisses. He was covered with the finest robe and given a celebration to rejoice he was home again. Our father never wants us to escape his love and when we do, his love for us never ceases. He watches for us to return to him eagerly. And when we do, He delights in our return.

Lord, I am truly amazed at your love for me. What is man that you should be mindful of us? I thank you that you will never let me go. I am forever grateful that your love for me never dies nor grows dim. Thank you for finding me in that pit of despair, pulling me out and placing me on level ground. Call the angels back, Lord. I am home again.

"But we had to celebrate and be glad, for this brother of yours was dead and is alive again; he was lost and is found." *(Luke 15:24)*

Do Not Measure by the Worlds Standards

My red-headed daughter was crying as she told me she did not think she was anything. She was in those awkward years as a young teenager and feeling all the despair that often besets our young ones growing up in a world where excessive competition meets peer pressure and the messages of the culture present role models that appear impossibly perfect and unobtainable in every physical manner. "I am not the prettiest one or the smartest one in my class," she said as she began the litany of perceived imperfections. "I am not the best at anything," she sobbed. How well I understood as I had cried the same things growing up. It was as if we do not value ourselves unless we beat all our competition. We compare ourselves to all of those around us and if we do not measure up, we do not make the cut. We use artificial standards to see if we are of value.

I knew my daughter, Jennifer, well enough to know many of her strengths and weaknesses. My love for her was not because of any perceived greatness nor diminished by any weakness. My love for her was because she was my baby girl, flesh of my flesh, bone of my bone, connected in both in the physical and spiritual worlds. She is mine. That alone makes her irreplaceable and infinitely valuable to me.

I wondered how to make her understand that her value was not in the physical world. Her true value was in who she is, not what she looked like or how intelligent or how athletic she was. Until we understand who we are to God above, we do not see our true priceless nature. And the world is always eager to tell us how we do not measure up.

It was a fourth grade school teacher that thought Einstein had a below average I.Q.. Oprah Winfrey was fired from her television job as a reporter because her employer did not think she was good enough on television. Thomas Edison was deemed outright stupid by his teachers. Marilyn Monroe was told to be a secretary because agents felt she was not good enough to be a model.

God told us, He does not look at the outside but looks at who we truly are as He looks into our hearts. The heart of the matter is the reality of the matter. We are made in his image – connected to him in both the physical and spiritual worlds. We are his babies and we are irreplaceable and infinitely loved and valued by him. He knows our weakness and strengths and still loves and wants us. He knows our sins and still loves us and offers us rescue from them. Do not give up. God makes things happen. You are valuable to Him and that is all that counts.

"I have seen something else under the sun. The race is not to the swift, or the battle to the strong, nor does food come to the wise, or wealth to the brilliant, or favor to the learned; but time and chance happen to them all." *(Ecclesiastes 9:11)*

"But the Lord said to Samuel, 'Do not consider his appearance or his height, for I have rejected him. The Lord does not look at the things man looks at. Man looks at the outward appearance, but the Lord looks at the heart.'" *(1 Samuel 16:7)*

Some of those who did not quit.[*]

Beethoven's teachers felt he was hopeless at music and would never succeed with the violin or in composing, yet he composed some of the best-loved symphonies of all time and 5 of them while he was completely deaf.

Enrico Caruso was told by his teachers he had no voice yet he became one of the best opera singers of our time.

Winston Churchill flunked the 6th grade and was defeated in every election for public office until the age of 62.

The Beatles were initially rejected by recording studios who did not like their sound.

As a penniless, divorced mother, raising a child on her own, J.K.Rowlings had 12 publishers reject her manuscripts before the 13th agreed to publish the first of the Harry Potter series.

Unable to talk until he was 4 years of age, Einstein's parents and teachers thought he was mentally handicapped.

Walt Disney was fired by a news editor because he felt Disney lacked imagination. Legend has it that he was turned down 302 times before getting financing for Disney World.

When Colonel Sanders, founder of KFC, retired at the age of 65, his first social security check came in for $105 dollars. Angry that he could not live off of it, he

---

[*] *Planet Motivation.* Copyright© 2009. <www.planetmotivation. com/never-**quit**.html>

decided to sell his fried chicken recipe. He drove around the country, knocking on doors, sleeping in his car, wearing his white suit. He got turned down 1,009 times before someone said 'yes'.

Vincent Van Gogh only sold one painting in his entire lifetime and that was to a friend. Now his works are worth millions.

Denied admission to the prestigious University of Southern California film school, Steven Spielberg enrolled in Cal State U. After directing some of the biggest blockbusters in history, he received an honorary degree from the university that rejected him.

Michael Jordan was cut from his high school basketball team.

Dr. Seuss's first book was rejected 27 times. John Grisham's first book was rejected 28 times. Stephen King's first book, *Carrie*, was rejected 30 times after which he threw the manuscript in the trash. His wife pulled it out and encouraged him to try again. He has sold over 350 million copies of his books.

Mark Cuban, the billionaire owner of the NBA's Dallas Mavericks got rich from the sale of his company Yahoo for $5.9 billion in stock. He admitted he was terrible at his early jobs and failed many times. He said, "I've learned that it doesn't matter how many times you failed, you only have to be right once. I tried to sell powdered milk. I was an idiot lots of times and learned from them all."

One thing that all successful people have in common. Even though they failed more than once, they did not quit.

Mom Grows Up

I am embarrassed to say that it took nearly 13 years for me to see Collin rather than the genetic problem of Downs Syndrome. I kept looking for normalcy instead of looking at the boy. It is not that I did not love him more than my own life. I lived on a dual edge of anxiety, worrying about his problems and looking at how he was different from others. It is just that I kept looking at his issues instead of his unique beauty. Some seemed to see it, but I could not. I was always challenged to bring him up as a 'normal' child when in fact he was wonderful already in spite of not being 'normal.' It was just in a way I refused to see. I wanted to measure him to a standard he would never be able to fulfill. I read the stories of vacations in Holland instead of Italy. I heard others say, "I would not change a thing about my special needs child." I just could not understand it. All I could think was, "ARE YOU PEOPLE CRAZY?"

I do not know exactly when my thinking changed or when I really saw Collin as who he truly is. I kept praying for healing of his condition but for Collin and me, the true healing was my being able to let Collin be Collin. It is not that he will never be healed. He will. If not in this world then in the Resurrection. The healing that was needed was more in me than Collin. I had to stop holding him up to an unrealistic model. And is not that what I did to myself as well? I was never perfect enough in my own mind. I compared myself, and still do, to thin models who I am sure never enjoy a good piece of pizza and a bowl of ice cream.

I compare myself to my more intelligent and accomplished siblings. I am not seeing me. My prayer had to change from, "Lord, change me" to "Lord let me see myself as you see me."

God does not make mistakes. Where I might think, "Lord, these hips of mine, what were you thinking?" The Lord sees the beautiful person he created. When I hold myself up to others, He holds me up by myself as his child as any loving parent lifts their child into the air above their heads in sheer joy. When did we ever come to the point in our childhood and adulthood where we decided we had to compare ourselves rather than love ourselves? To become more like Christ, is to love yourself and others, and not to pick out failings and ugliness. Our Father in Heaven will change us as we need to be changed. It is only in becoming the beloved child and trusting him to love us exactly where and in what condition he finds us that He can finish the good work he started in us. Blessed Mother Teresa of Calcutta said, "God doesn't call us to be successful. He calls us to be faithful." We really are a work in progress!

Now when Collin hugs me and kisses me, in only the way a Down's child of 16 can do, I think, "I would not change him." (Well, maybe I would change his packing suitcases issue but that is another story for another day.) God gave to me the most loving of children to reflect his love for me. Oh Loving Father in heaven, finish in me the good work you started and let me see myself and others as you see us.

"Trust in the Lord with all of your heart and lean not on your own understanding; in all your ways acknowledge him and he will make your paths straight." *(Proverbs 3:5-6)*

Don Juan, Collin

Collin was becoming a regular Don Juan around the ladies. He bragged at having three girlfriends to his brothers and sister. Lucy was a favorite. They met in TASK sports (Team Activities for Special Kids*). But Lucy lives a long way from us, on the other side of TASK's service area and is in school with other TASK kids. It was inevitable that Lucy would start dating and dating others in school with her and closer to her home.

So when Lucy and Jack became girlfriend-boyfriend, Collin was crushed. He got in the car after soccer one day and said, "I am so jealous of Jack." He was hurt and refused to talk about it. If I tried to say something, he got angry. So we drove in silence almost the entire way home. There is that point in your life as a child's mother, where you cannot just kiss the hurts away and they no longer want you to hold them and calm them in their hurts and fears. You feel helpless at being unable to fix the problems or help them solve the issues at hand.

The Lord tells us how He longs to calm us as a child on their mother's lap. How even if we are forgotten by our mother and our father, He will never forget us. He tells us how he keeps every tear we shed in a bottle, so precious to him are our sorrows. He longs to gather us as a mother

---

* Note: *Team Activities for Special Kids* is a wonderful organization in St. Louis, MO dedicated to providing various sports and physical activities for special needs children. Visit www.tasksports.org. Names involved in story above have been changed.

hen gathers her children under her wings. He keeps watch at the window awaiting our return if we ever leave him. He knocks at our door hoping we will answer and let him in. If we who love our own children long to ease their pains, how much more must our Father in Heaven long to ease our pains? He longs to wipe every tear from our eyes. How many times has His love for us been rejected? Who knows better that pain and yet still reaches out to us?

As we neared our home, we were stopped at a red light. I turned to Collin and said, "I know how you feel. I once loved someone and they did not love me back." Collin was surprised and wanted to know all about it. We cannot change the feelings or push them out of our hearts. All we could do was share them and know that we have a Father in Heaven who truly understands. We must remember this and pray doubly hard for those who reject the Father.

"For we do not have a high priest who is unable to sympathize with our weaknesses, but we have one who has been tempted in every way, just as we are-yet was without sin. Let us then approach the throne of grace with confidence, so we may receive mercy and find grace to help us in our time of need." (Hebrews 4:15-16)

I See You, not Your Messes

When Collin was learning to feed himself, and this was true for all of my children, it was a given that food would be about everywhere. He would smear it on the high chair table, on his face and even in his hair. Every meal was a guaranteed cleaning task. One could only hope the mess was confined to the kitchen and not everywhere and on everyone. I could not even imagine being upset about it since what would one expect? If any of the kids were 18 years of age and still making that kind of mess, there might be some motherly anger, but as babies, you could laugh and hope that they grew out of it soon. And it was a teaching process where gentle correction was required. I have a number of pictures with each child sitting in the high chair with food all over them. I plan to show the pictures at various high points in their life. I would never condemn them for something they were not aware of or could not help due to their age or inexperience. I never expected them to be perfect, but in their innocent imperfection I found great joy. I would surround them with my love and clean them up. When I look at them today, I do not see the messes they made.

I really wish that all of the messes I have created were as innocent as a baby trying to feed themselves. But some of my innocent messes, Satan has used to bring me down in an attempt to steal my joy. "Why did you say that" or "How could you be so dumb," were refrains that often filled my subconscious and robbed me of inner peace.

Mary Lytton

It was easier to forgive others their innocent mistakes than it was for me to forgive and forget mine. It did not seem possible that God would see me as an innocent baby learning to feed myself getting food everywhere and needing to be cleaned up afterwards. He would have to teach me but not as an angry father demanding perfection but as a loving father seeing my abilities and laughing, yes even laughing at some of the situations I would manage to get myself into, knowing full well that when all was said and done, He was still there to clean me up and give me another chance. When He looks at us, He does not see us and our messes but the One who surrounds us. Our failures are real, but Christ's victory over all the sin and death in our life is secure. I just hope that my Father in heaven did not take pictures to show everyone when I get there.

"Therefore, there is now no condemnation for those who are in Christ Jesus." *(Romans 8:1)*

"You prepare a table before me in the presence of my enemies." *(Psalm 23:5)*

Adventures with Collin

A few years ago, I decided to take Collin to the movies to see "Curious George." I had no idea that the movie was about my life with Collin and that I would enjoy it more that he did.

You see, this boring Archeologist named Ted, or the guy in the yellow hat, goes in search of a wondrous treasure and ends with up with something he never expected.

The little monkey, George, is so innocent and so naïve that he has no concept of danger. His curiosity leads him into all sorts of adventures for which Ted must chase after him to protect him. George never even realizes when Ted is saving his life and keeping him from serious harm. Life for the man in the yellow hat is never the same and certainly never boring. He comes to realize the true treasure in his life is George. Like Ted, I am forever chasing after Collin, my unnoticed hands fixing the messes and trying to keep him safe. I would die to keep him safe. A speeding car, a madman with a gun or a burning building would not stop me from attempting to save him even if it meant my own life. I would not even have to think about it. It would just happen because love refuses to quit. He is my treasure.

I like to think that I am the one in control of everything. That my life as the person in the yellow hat is handling all the disasters that come our way. In reality, we are all curious George.

How many times have we had to say, "Wow, that was a lucky thing", as we watched cars zip by that would have hit us if something had not diverted our attention? Or how many times has something happened that seemed like a terrible disaster to us at the time and then later we realize if that had not happened something worse would have? How many people do we know that have gone to the doctor for one small problem only to have them find a bigger one that needed immediate attention? We probably do not even realize 90% of the time when the hand of God is working to save us, to lovingly guide us to safety, holding us when we are sad and protecting us from unseen danger. God, our Father, treasures us. Where your heart is, there will be your treasure. He treasures us so much, He sent his son, Jesus, to die for us, to save us from the ultimate death. He never quits trying because Love refuses to quit. He never says, "I've had enough of you." Never. He is Love, true pure Love and it never fails. He even sends his angels to watch over us.

Accept His Love this day, freely given. Then, as He leads you, enjoy the adventure. And maybe try to stay out of danger and give the angels He puts over you a break.

"The heavens declare the glory of God: the skies proclaim the work of his hands." *(Psalm 19:1)*

Thou Shalt Not Smoke

There are times when we see our children make some very bad decisions. When they are children, it is our job to train them in the way they should go so that when they are old, they will not depart from the teachings. But that does not mean they always will stay the course and as adults we have little power to make them get back on track with what we believe is best for them. They will decide for themselves no matter what we say or do. Which is why, when I found out my son, Ben, had taken up smoking, I was overcome with frustration and sorrow.

Smoking is a big issue with me. I watched as several loved ones died of lung cancer. It is an ugly death and I never want to see any of my children suffer that way. I tried when they were small to explain how terrible lung cancer was and how smoking caused it for my Uncle Jim and others. But of course, Ben decided for himself he wanted to smoke. I never said this was the 11th commandment, "Thou shalt not smoke." But even if I had, it would never be because I am mean and do not want my children to have fun or to not enjoy smoking or to not look cool or any of a hundred reasons someone might give as reasons they want to smoke. It is because I believe it eventually ruins one's health. Since I deeply love Ben, it is a consequence I do not want for him.

It deeply saddens me to see him smoke. I keep praying that Ben will quit before his health is destroyed and, no, his smoking does not mean I love him less, only that I pray and am watching him all the more.

How much more must it sadden our Father in heaven when we knowingly break his commandments? Not because He is a mean and controlling God, just the opposite! The commandments were created to bring peace and health and love to ourselves and our community. They would be a natural outcome of loving God with all our hearts and minds and souls and our neighbors as ourselves. When we do not love God or ourselves or one another in the way we should, we stumble over the commands and into sin. Every sin from big to small destroys the peace and joy around us. It ruins the health of our souls. Our Father must be very concerned for us when we stray away. Is that not why He would send his only begotten Son to die for our sins? It is not his wish that any should die in sin, but He vigilantly looks over us to bring us home again.

The most wonderful news is this, God gives us another chance every day. Today's sin is not the end! His mercy is renewed each morning – so that we can live life as He created our lives to be in love and harmony. I pray that we all can remember how much we are in need of his forgiveness and extend that forgiveness to ourselves and our neighbors.

"Because of the Lord's great love, we are not consumed, for his compassions never fail. They are new every morning." *(Lamentations 3:22-23)*

Do it with a Grateful Heart

Both my eldest children were complaining as they did their chores. Ben and Jennifer, who usually fought each other, were now united in defense against what they were calling "forced labor." Even my compliant child, Kenny, was watching to see what came of their complaints. His complaint would not be far behind if they succeeded in escaping their work. It seemed like it was easier for me to do the work myself than ask my children to chip in. However, even if it was easier, I knew they had to learn. If they never had anything asked of them, how would they learn to give? If they never had to do anything, how would they grow up to be productive people? If they had everything handed to them, how would they be able to be sympathetic to others who had far less or nothing at all? Compassion and mercy are learned in life. We all had to learn. How much more pleasant it is now when my children all grown up, ask, "What can we do to help?"

I remember how often I would find ways to not do what the Lord asked of me. "Why should I be nice to him? Did you hear what he said to me, Lord?" "Why should I give so much to the church, I need it more than they do?" "OH, you wanted me to do that, Lord?" (Like I really did not know) "Sorry, I forgot." "It's not fair." I am certain that our Father in heaven has heard every excuse under the sun. He did not create life to be fair. We live our lives to learn and grow into the children of God. I sometimes forget, "That if today you hear his voice, harden not your hearts." And "Here I am Lord, I've come to do your will." Easy to say. Tough to do. I guess we still have some growing in store for us.

Help me to remember, oh Lord, how it sounds like crying babies when I complain about the work you have given me to do. I am here because it is your will, this very place and this very time in history. Let me give all I have with a happy grateful heart!

"Remember this: Whoever sows sparingly will also reap sparingly, and whoever sows generously will also reap generously. Each man should give what he has decided in his heart to give, not reluctantly or under compulsion, for God loves a cheerful giver." *(2 Corinthians 9:6-7)*

Apple Picking

I thought Collin would enjoy picking apples with me as Eckert's had so many exciting things for kids to see and do. We took the wagon ride out to the orchard and true to form, Collin managed to run off from me amidst the rows of apple trees. I have no explanation for why I thought this would be any different from how he was at home. I just hoped he and I would have a fun day. I went searching for him and after 15 minutes of frantic running and calling, there he was down the hill several rows over, oblivious to everything around him except hundreds of trees and apples. Did he not know how dangerous it was to run away from his mother where anyone might snatch him or he might step on a snake or some other imagined danger? I was hot and tired as I directed him back to where I left the bag of apples I had picked and sat him down under the tree. I looked up at the apples above our head and said, "Why did you do this to me God?" Why was Collin born this way? Why does he have to be so difficult to care for? Why, God, Why? I loved going out to pick apples and here I was sitting under the trees, with the feeling of frustration and a sense of injustice flooding my heart. I just could not understand why and was angry at the unfairness of it all.

God did not answer.

I realize there were many times I ran off from the Lord to pursue my own thing. How many times he must have left the 99 behind to come find me and how frustrating I must have been – oblivious to everything around me and the dangers that lurked in the shadows. Did this happen because I so often wandered off from him?

Finally I thought, 'He knows that no matter what, love will pull me back.' I could never run away from my son; I would always go in search of him. And the Lord my God will be strong through me. He knows I will do what is needed but only if He gives me the strength to go on. He knows I would say, "Yes Lord," then proceed to give me the answers when I did not even know the questions. The truth is, I am weak and He is strong. No matter what comes, it is doable because He will do it through me. I just have to stop complaining long enough to see his hand in all things. I have to stop being the tired, frustrated mother dwelling in self-pity and be the mother who can do all things because God lives in me.

Laugh, because He dwells in you.

"For the eyes of the Lord range throughout the earth to strengthen those whose hearts are fully committed to him." *(2 Chronicles 16:9)*

A Home for You

When I was getting remarried, it seemed to affect Jennifer the hardest. We were moving to a new home in a new area and she would have to start at a new school as well. She was also not happy with having a step-father. I paid extra attention to making her room in the new house a special place for her. I got her a canopy bed and we picked out a wall paper border to put around the top of the wall. She got a new dresser. I did what I could to help her adjust to all the changes taking place and wanted her to feel that this was just as much her home as everyone else in the family. I wanted her to know she was loved. It really was not any different than when I was pregnant with Jennifer. I wanted to prepare the crib and baby blankets. I wanted to have little clothes ready for her. After our move, from time to time when she was upset, she would accuse me of not wanting her or that she felt the new house was not her home. I simply pointed out that I had done a lot to make a very special place for her because she was mine and I wanted her with me.

She was no different than me. How many times did I accuse the Lord of not wanting me? Out of fear, so often I thought myself without a place in this world. In his book, *A Severe Mercy,* Sheldon Vanauken, in his correspondence with C.S. Lewis, quotes Lewis as saying, "Do fish complain of the sea for being wet? Or if they did, would that fact itself not strongly suggest that they had not always been, or would not always be, purely aquatic creatures? ...... If you are really a product of a materialistic universe, how is it you don't feel at home there?" And maybe that is exactly the point. This really is not our true home, now is it?

At the Last Supper, Jesus comforts His disciples by telling them that He goes before them to prepare a room for them. "In my Father's house, there are many rooms," He tells them. There is a place for us. A home where we are to live with God forever. A place fixed up especially just for us. He wants us with him because He loves us and we are his. Even before I was born, He was designing my room in his mansion. If I, who am imperfect, love my children enough to give them a home and make it special just for them, how much more will Father God prepare a place for us? He has already prepared a place for you and me. As I leave this world, I hope I remember to say, "Have the angels prepare my room Father, I am coming home!"

I Love the Sound of Your Laughter

I was folding clothes in the bedroom when I heard the voices of my children in the kitchen. Their stream of laughter seemed to pour out of the room and saturated the entire house. My older children were home for Thanksgiving and they were all sitting around the computer, showing Collin funny internet videos of kittens and puppies. I just had to join them to see what was so funny. Their laughter was more beautiful than any musical composition. The tempo was contagious and I never wanted to hear it end. As a parent, nothing makes me happier than to see my children happy. The love they shared with one another was centered on Collin. Their love for Collin allowed them to become childlike with him and prevailed against all their adult worries and fears for one special moment in time. Just remembering it now, brings the melody of their laughter back to my heart.

Sometimes I think, we forget that God our Father wants us to be happy and joyful. I sometimes think of Him as the dour parent who only notices when I am being bad. Do we think of him as the loving parent who longs for laughter and takes great pride in our ability to put aside for a time all of our worries and fears and just spend a moment in time in sheer joy with one another?

When we laugh together in love, God is there with us enjoying our laughter and laughing with us. He longs for us to be joyful. He loves to hear us laugh.

Today we need to quiet ourselves as a weaned child on our mother's lap and laugh with joy. Our Father laughs with us.

"Sarah said, 'God has brought me laughter, and everyone who hears about this will laugh with me.'" *(Genesis 21:6)*

I Call You by Name

In the long months of waiting for my babies to be born, one of the more important tasks my husbands and I had was to pick out a name. It was quite a task to find one we both agreed on, and since we did not always know for sure the sex of our baby, we had to find both a girl and a boy's name. Baby books were searched, lists were made and meanings of the names were scrutinized. Names are so terribly important. Then when my babies were born, we sent out announcements telling the world that our little one, by name, was here. In Baptism, their name was announced to the church, and by their name, they would be baptized in the name of the Father, the Son and the Holy Spirit.

In the ancient Hebrew times, the naming of the baby was a ceremony where the newborn was placed on his father's lap. Lifting the child for all to see, the father would announce the name for all to hear. By this act, the father declared his acceptance of the child as his own. In our culture, the father's last name is usually given to the child as their last name, telling the community, that this child belongs to his family.

How many times did God change the names of his chosen ones? Abram to Abraham, Sarai to Sarah, Saul to Paul, Simon to Peter. The list is very long, and in fact, we all will be given a true name, the name God the Father chose for us before we even came to be. Then each of us will be drawn to our Father's lap and He will take us in his arms and announce his special name He gave to us for all to hear. He will declare we are his own.

"I have summoned you by name, you are mine." *(Isaiah 43:1)*

"To he who overcomes, I will give some of the hidden manna, I will also give him a white stone with a new name written on it, known only to him who receives it." *(Revelation 2:17)*

Tom meets his new born son, Ken.

Politics

Upon hearing about the actions of someone we knew, my daughter once asked, "Adults act like that?" My children seemed to be surprised as they grew up how babyish many adults could be. She and her siblings were always vying for attention or fighting to get their own way or working to express dominance over each other. Selfishness is a trade mark of children. She understood that of herself and her brothers, but adults? Yes, beautiful girl, some adults never grow up.

I would love to tell you that I was a perfect parent and that I never had children that fought. (HA!) Or that I could say that I had children willing to compete to express their love for one another. (NOT.) Or that they were humble and willing to give into each other needs. (WOW, I wish). But my children were real children who had to grow up and learn how to treat others. And the hardest job I ever had was raising my children. I was never the perfect parent who always got it right. I failed them many times. But, they get it now that they are grown in spite of themselves and me. They have since put away their childish behavior and put on the cloak of adulthood. They no longer walk as children and speak as children. They came to realize there was more to growing up than getting bigger, they had to learn to share and put others first. Blaming mom for their failures is not an option.

So when many people were speaking about politics in the work place, in schools, or in their church, I begin to wonder if they never gave up on the childish notion of 'me first'. Of all places, the church should be where egos are put aside and humility reigns as we work to outdo each other in acts of kindness and love. There should be compromise in the areas that are not deadly and a wish to see each other thrive even at the risk of being overlooked ourselves. Mercy and forgiveness should be in the arsenal of our spiritual warehouse. It is like all the sheep want to be the shepherd but only if they get to pick the herd otherwise they will go off to be a herd of one. And even the most perfect parent, God in heaven, can apparently have the most wayward children.

When we find ourselves in the mist of 'politics', it becomes necessary that we first check our own motives and desires. If they are not in line with Christ, then the battle for our 'soul' begins there, not with others. Have we put away our childish behavior and no longer walk and talk like children? We are all the sheep and Christ is our shepherd. Lead us Lord in the way we should go, for you alone have the words of eternal life.

"Therefore, as God's chosen people, holy and dearly loved, clothe yourselves with compassion, kindness, humility, gentleness and patience. Bear with each other and forgive whatever grievances you may have against one another." *(Colossians 4:12)*

Going it Alone

I remember one particularity difficult time while raising three young children on my own. I read the scripture, "Come to me, all you who are weary and burdened and I will give you rest. Take my yoke upon you, and learn from me; for I am gentle and humble in heart, and you will find rest for your souls. For my yoke is easy and my burden is light." *(Matthew 11:28)*

I thought wearily, "Lord, this doesn't make any sense to me." I was struggling and worrying and hurting and no matter what I did, it never seemed to be enough. Not big enough, good enough, or enough in any way. I was trying so hard and tired of never really making the grade.

I became angry at our Lord, imagine that, and said, "I don't know why I have to be so great when you already are!"

That is when I had one of those moments, when it felt as if the Lord swooped down and picked me up to hug me. In that moment, He was telling me that I finally got it. I had been trying to do everything on my own. That is why it was hard. I had been trying to be perfect by myself. No wonder I was failing.

He never intended me to carry the burden by myself.

He never intended for me to be good on my own or perfect by my own hand. All of that is impossible. He never asked me to do the impossible. He intended to do it through me. So that only in him could I brag. So that only in Him could the impossible be possible. Only in Him could I do all things.

That's when everything got easy. OK, easier.

Sometimes, I still try to go it alone. I am reminded very quickly of how hard that is. Looking for sympathy, I may still complain. Silly me. If I had not been so stubborn in my quest to kick against the goad, I would have been a lot happier.

Happy Christians understand the yoke of Christ. Go out and be happy today!

What He Wants for Us

It seemed very hard to believe when Collin finally turned 16. "Could it be that it was that long since he was born," I remember thinking. And like most of his birthdays, there is always a sadness in my heart when I go shopping for birthday gifts. For my other children, 16 was a 'rite of passage.' They could get their driver's license and exercise a certain amount of freedom extended to mature teens. For Collin, the difference in what he would love as a birthday gift and what he can actually have are magnified each passing year. He would love to drive. But that is not possible right now. Even if he would study and actually pass the written exam and maybe even the driving test, his safety is foremost in my heart. What he wants just might kill him. So that which he would love the most, I cannot give him. I want more than anything to make him happy and give him what he really wants. This is the source of my sadness. I think, "Collin, How I long to make your greatest dreams come true." Someday, we may be able to prepare him in such a way that he can have those things he longs for the most. For now, other things will have to suffice.

Our Father in heaven loves us more than I could ever love my own children. He knows each of us intimately and knows exactly what we can handle and that which would destroy us. How much more He must long to fulfill our dreams. How much more must He long to give us our heart's desire. Our Lord is the source of all riches. His words created every valuable thing in the universe. There is nothing He cannot give. If you are asking for something and believing, I do believe God will find a way to give it to you. "What so ever you ask for in faith, you will receive," as long as you, "Seek me first, and I will grant you the desires of your heart," He tells us. It just may be, that He will have to prepare you for what you are asking from him. For now, His grace must suffice. Accept His grace as he prepares you for your heart's desire.

Just do not be afraid to ask, then wait for His reply.

The Test

Collin was in a bad mood because I had him stop playing his video game and unload the dishwasher. To my demand for his obedience, I had to add the threat of grounding as well. As he slammed the Tupperware into the cabinet, he was upset because the bowls and lids were not staying in the cabinet but falling out repeatedly all over the floor. It just made him all the more upset and for some strange reason, he felt that yelling at the bowls would help. I was much too busy to intervene, so I called out to him, "Do it right or you will do it again." That seemed to quiet him down even though I am sure the bowls and lids were not put away correctly and it took him three times as long to complete the task because he was constantly having to pick up what fell down. If only he would do it right the first time.

Our lives are full of daily lessons. St. Theresa of Avila once said that it is as if we were placed here to learn not to make the same mistakes as the angels who rebelled against God. That means to learn to trust him, obey him and do whatever He asks with a happy heart. How many times have I had to redo lessons in order to do them right? If only my mistakes were with plastic bowls and lids. Some things I can never re-do correctly as the people are gone and now it is too late. How many times have I exclaimed, "OH NO not again!" Joyce Meyer said, that it was only an eleven day journey from Egypt to the Promised Land but it took the Israelites forty years to get there because they had to learn to do it right. They needed a change of heart and a new way of thinking.

Today I pray, that if you need me to do something, Father God, that you will let me hear from you loud and clear and that your grace will enable to me to do it with a happy heart, willing and wanting to please you. Today, I want to ace the test and graduate to something better.

"For he chose us in him before the creation of the world to be holy and blameless in his sight. In love he predestined us to be adopted as his sons through Jesus Christ, in accordance with his pleasure and will." *(Ephesians 1:4-5)*

Gratitude from a Joyful Heart

One of the traits of Down's syndrome children is that they are so affectionate. People do not realize what a blessing in disguise these loving children can be. Collin has no idea how to hide his feelings. When I come home from the grocery store every week, I know that Collin will be at the door to help me bring in the groceries. Any item he likes that is contained within the bags, and there is always something he loves from cereal to milk, he is overjoyed and hugs me with endless gratitude. A new bottle of shampoo in hand and I am greeted with hugs and kisses. You would have thought I bought him a motorcycle or have given him a trip to Disney World. I cannot help but laugh at his expression of thankfulness over the littlest of things. He never gets tired of the hugs and thanks. I never get tired of his excitement and joy. His joy and gratitude over even the simplest of things is humbling to my soul.

How often have I thanked my heavenly Father for my daily bread? We seem to take for granted how He provides for us. Blessing become rituals before meals, something to get done before we eat. How often have we sat down and really taken stock of all that He gives us. Each day we wake, we should thank him for life that we can get up for the day, instead of thinking, OH GOD the alarm went off and I have to get up to go to work. (Oh, I never say that…☺) We should never tire of thanking him that we have warm homes and beds to rise from and food to eat. We should be exuberant to be living in a wonderful country where food is abundant. How incredible is the number of things we have for which to be thankful. If I, who am imperfect, can smile knowing how thankful over every little thing my child will be, how much more will our Heavenly Father smile knowing how excited and thankful we will be at His gifts? Let us make Him smile this day by getting really excited and thankful over all He provides!

"Sing to the Lord with thanksgiving; make music to our God on the harp." *(Psalm 147:7)*

"But let all who take refuge in you be glad; let them ever sing for joy." *(Psalm 5:11)*

I Will Be Your Landing Spot if You Fall

When Collin was small, he was transferred to a grade school further from home, due to some of his behavior issues. The bus ride was a lot longer and as always, Collin would fall asleep. One day when I met his bus, things almost took a tragic turn. I climbed the stairs up into the bus and picked him up to carry him home since he was sound asleep. When I turned to go back down, my feet were off balance with Collin and his backpack and I started to fall down the stairs with Collin in my arms. I did not have time to think about it or decide, I knew instinctively that I was **not** going to fall on my child, if anything, I would turn and let him fall on top of me. In a split second action, I jerked my body around to fall backwards and my foot became untangled landing squarely on the next step down. Somehow by the grace of God and the help of angels, neither one of us fell or were hurt. Though the bus driver and I were shaken, Collin merely woke up from his nap. I had no qualms of any kind that I should be his cushion if we fell. And I know that I am no different from most of the moms and dads on the face of this earth. What is truly incredible is that in the blink of an eye, we can sense danger to our children and act accordingly, even if it means our own life is put at stake. We do not hesitate nor would we even say after the fact, "Why did I do that?" We will put ourselves in the wake of personal danger to protect our babies even to the point of losing our own lives. It is the wondrous miraculous binding of love.

We can only wonder, how many times did we awake from our sleep, unknowing that our Father in heaven was protecting us from imminent danger? He whose love for us towers above the heavens, watches over us and His love cannot be exceeded by our own. St. Catherine of Siena once said, "Nails were not enough to hold God–and–man nailed and fastened on the cross, had not love held him there." The love that can withstand any and all suffering is the same kind of love that ties us to our children. It is an image of the love of our Father in heaven who sets His Divine Mercy as an answer to the very gates of hell. If we fall, we can be assured that He will be our landing spot.

"When I say, 'My foot is slipping,' your love, Lord, supported me. When anxiety was great within me, your consolation brought joy to my soul." *(Psalm 94:18-19)*

Fighting Again?

It was one of those days, and as a widow with three little children, I seemed to have a lot of those days. I had to go to the hardware store and although I like the hardware store, it usually meant I had to fix something that I did not know anything about. Dragging the kids with me was no picnic for them or for me and of course they chose that time to start a fight. It seemed that one child was taking more room in the cart than the other child thought they should have. I tried to get them to be quiet without much luck. Looking up, I saw a women from my widowed support group who had taken offense at me. Desperate to not look like a totally incompetent mother in front of her, I tried even harder to keep the children quiet. My anger got the better of me and when we got in the car, I angrily said to them, "Don't you know how you make us look in public with that fighting. There are people in there that know us. There was a lady who doesn't like me and you made me look like a terrible mother." I was hurt by how their behavior reflected on me as their mother. Their fighting was over silly kid things. Things that if they really thought about it, they would even agree, in the long scheme of things it really doesn't matter. Why is it so hard for kids to show the world how much they really love each other? Isn't it really a choice? "What looks better, guys? Kids who are fighting or kids who are making the best of things and choosing to get along," I asked them.

I know I did not handle the situation very well. I got angry with them when they were just children. After all, how many times have I fought with my brothers not caring how it looked to others? There were probably some people present who had taken offense at my Father God and thought, "Look how his children behave. They are no better than the rest of the world!" How many times have I grieved my Father's heart with things that in the long scheme, really do not matter? Or with issues that were covering deeper problems and preventing me from digging down to discover the plight that really needed a solution or a healing?

He leads me on the path of righteousness for his name sake, that I might be worthy to call him Father God. He created us to reflect his glory and his character. Sometimes I forget that I need to choose his will over mine and his plan over my plan. When others offend me, I need to be the strong one in Christ and forgive. How can fighting with my brothers lead others to Christ? When my brother fights with me, I need to say, "I still love you". Every day we are given the challenge to reflect God's holiness in us or reflect our own desires and fears. What looks better, God's reflection or our reflection? How I long for the presence of God to radiate through me for all to see. Father God, thank you for being so patient with me.

"For he chose us in him before the creation of the world to be holy and blameless in his sight. In love He predestined us to be adopted as his sons through Jesus Christ, in accordance with his pleasure and will – to the praise of his glorious grace, which He has freely given us in the One He loves." *(Ephesians 1:4-5)*

I can Pick You out of the Crowd

Ben's graduation from high school was a major milestone for all of our family. The ceremony was held in a huge auditorium due to the size of the graduating class. There were well over 200 students and 6 times that number of teachers and family members who all assembled for that special moment in time. We were sitting high in the bleachers yet I could still find Ben in the crowd. They were all wearing the same black cap and gowns but I knew my son and memorized where he was sitting. It did not matter that there were hundreds of other students. That one was my son and I would never let him be 'lost' in the crowd. I would never say, "There is just too many people to pay attention to the one student." No, I was there to see my son graduate and I would not miss this moment for anything. I was there to cheer him on as they called his name. To this day, I remember each of my children's graduations from high school and college. I remember where they sat and where I was sitting. And I remember how I could not wait to celebrate their achievements.

When the millions assemble to worship Our Lord and Savior, at his throne in heaven, He will look for each of us in the crowd. If the Lord our God created every star in the sky and calls them by name so how much more will He look for us in the crowd. It doesn't matter that millions are assembled, He knows each of us and has a special name for us which He will call and cheer us on as we enter His Kingdom. Eye has not seen nor ear has heard the awesome wonders of the Kingdom that our Lord has prepared for us ahead of time. We will not be lost nor forgotten in the crowd.

"He determines the number of the stars and calls them each by name. Great is Our Lord and mighty in power; his understanding has no limit." *(Psalm 147:4-5)*

No One Left Behind

It had to be one of my biggest 'mama' failures in memory. There were two car loads of family members leaving from my house to go to Six Flags together. I was leading the caravan and got three miles from home when at a stop light, I looked back and saw that the baby car seat was empty. "Where is Kenny," I called to the kids in the back. They said, "He's not here." I pulled over and searched the other car. Fear close to terror filled my heart. "Where is KENNY?" is all I could think about. I turned the car around and must have broken a few speed limits to get back. What if he got hurt as we left and we did not know it? Was he in the house or on the driveway? How could I have driven off without noticing he was not in car? Every mother's worst imagined fear gripped me and I knew I would have walked through fire to get home to him. No band of bears and lions would have stopped me, even if they had existed in Ballwin, MO, and certainly I would have faced an army as well. As I drove into the driveway, I saw his little sad face looking out the front window. It still brings tears to my eyes. Relief flooded me as I saw he was OK, only saddened by being left behind. I wrapped him in my arms and scooped him up. We both cried then dried our tears and went on to a happy fun day. Thank God!

If I, who am such a silly forgetful mother at times, would refuse to be stopped in finding my lost child afraid for his safety and well-being, how much more must our Lord be when for whatever reason he discovers we are not with him. It would never have even been a remote thought to think, oh well, I got everyone else in the car. Or say, I guess he just missed the ride, too bad. So how was it that when I was growing up, I often thought that I might not matter to God, after all, He has so many other children who are better in so many ways. I did not know that He heard my cries of fear and loneliness and would mount a cloud and come down to rescue me. I did not know that he would repel armies to save me. I did not really understand that His Son's death on the cross was as much for me as it was everyone else. I was almost afraid to accept the salvation He offered out of fear of offending Him. It is never His will that anyone should be left behind. I would have to go through many experiences before I understood. And I would have to have become a mother, myself, to fully see how much I meant to Him.

Where could I go that I could hide from Him? If I go down into the pit, He would be there or up into the heaven, He would find me. Even if my own mother and father were to forget me, He would never forget.

If you are like me and do not fully understand God's love for you, please know this above all things today. There are no stepchildren, cousins, aunts, uncles, grandchildren or slaves in God's house. We are all his children. And He loves each of us infinitely. I, too, often ask, "What are we, in our lowly human state, that You dear God care of us?" It is a mystery of love I wish to explore for all eternity.

"What is man that you are mindful of him, the son of man that you care for him? You made him a little lower than the heavenly beings and crowned him with glory and honor." *(Psalm 8:4-5)*

Tests of the Heart

Collin's early school years proved to be incredibly difficult for the school, teachers and his family all combined. His behavior was sometimes more than we could bear and for the school it was unacceptable. Disciplinarily notes led to suspensions led to parent-teacher conferences. Collin was transferred to different schools two times. Every time the phone rang at work, I would cringe and pray, "Dear God do not let this be about something else Collin did today at school." I wanted the very best for Collin and each transfer meant Collin would be in a school further and further away from home. Each set back was more and more heartbreaking. We talked to Collin – all of us, parents, brothers and sisters. We resorted to different drug therapies to try and help. God forgive us, it was horrible. More often than not, we were on our knees in prayer. The IEP before the final move was almost more than I could handle. We were told, Collin had to go to the inclusive Special School where they had padded rooms if needed. We wanted with all of our hearts for Collin to thrive and excel and be happy. Never would it have occurred to me that since he was imperfect with Down's syndrome, I should abandon him to return to strictly caring for my more 'perfect' children. Collin had no idea the lengths we went to help him.

I tell you this only because it taught me the lengths a parent would go through to help their child. These tests of the heart are by no means the most difficult a parent can face but if we who are imperfect moms and dads would agonize to love, protect and defend our children, how much more must our heavenly Father agonize over each and every one of us. In one man's near death experience, he asked Jesus if the saddest day in heaven was the day Jesus died on the cross and Jesus told him, "No, the saddest day in heaven is the final judgment." On that day, so many of God's children will be turned away from heaven and Jesus said, "On that day, all of heaven will hear his Father cry." Each and every child and each and every one of us matters to our Father in heaven. We have no idea the lengths He went and will go through to keep us close to him. We do not truly understand all He went through to save us even when we see his Son on the cross.

I have been blessed to see the miracle of Collin's healing. His behavior changed and his personality blossomed. God has been very good to me!

"Jesus said, 'Let the little children come to me, and do not hinder them: for the kingdom of heaven belongs to such as these." *(Matthew 19:14)*

"The righteous cry out, and the Lord hears them: he delivers them from all their troubles." *(Psalm 34:17)*

My Children know my Voice

It seemed like it took a long time for me to teach Collin about the dangers of going with strangers. I had to keep a very watchful eye on him for a very long time. I would never have dreamed of letting him play in the street to learn for himself how dangerous that sort of activity can be. I would never do that because the lesson might very well have killed him. There are just some things in life that are too important for children to learn on their own. For his own safety, I had to teach him to avoid strangers and keep him out of the street. It wasn't because I was being mean. I must say 'NO' sometimes out of the greatest of love. Life is fraught with seemingly endless arrays of dangers that children have no idea about. It is my duty as his mother to educate him for his own safety. Who would be the most vigilant out of love if not me? Whose voice should he trust for his safety? Likewise, if I would not step aside to let someone else parent him, why would I ever abdicate my spiritual authority over my son? It is also my job to teach him about Christ so that his spiritual life may be saved.

Jesus tells us that his sheep know his voice. A shepherd understood that. A shepherd would teach the baby lambs the sound of his voice so that no matter what flock they were grazing with, when the shepherd wanted to take his flock somewhere else, he had only to call and they would follow. None of the other sheep would come to the shepherd's voice, only those belonging to his flock would come. The good shepherd would even lay down his life for his flock. If we do not teach our children with love the sound of the shepherds' voice, some other power will come to lead them away. They will follow whatever voice calls to them, even the voice of destruction.

Someday, my son will be an adult and when my voice fades, I pray he knows the voice of Jesus so as to never be without his shepherd.

"I am the good shepherd; I know my sheep and my sheep know me-just as the Father knows me and I know the Father- and I lay down my life for the sheep." *(John 10:14-15)*

I Will Feed You

I felt like I was always cooking either breakfast, lunch or dinner. I would just clean up one meal and my little ones were hungry again. "Mom, I'm hungry," seemed like the second most common refrain, just after the complaint, "Mom, he (or she) did this." I would never think to tell them, go feed yourselves. It was my job to feed them and I took that seriously. Besides, telling them to do it themselves when they were little – you just never knew what they could get into and what they might eat. So when it came time for them to receive their First Communion, I was filled with pride and satisfaction that I had managed to get them to the table of the Lord. The food I would give them might last a few hours, but the food of Our Lord is for a life time. Following them up to receive Communion, I remember praying, "Give me more time, Lord, and I will get them all up here." I would no more allow them to starve to death physically than I would prevent them from being fed spiritually. I would no more tell my babies, "Go feed yourself," than I would tell them to find salvation on their own. I know it is my job to lead them to Christ, who prepares a table before us.

What an awesome gift our Father in Heaven gives us. He takes His job to feed us very seriously. He fed them in the desert with manna from Heaven and He feeds us now on the bread of Life, the Word of God made flesh. He did not leave us here for our souls to suffer starvation, for truly his flesh became real food and his blood real drink and whoever eats his flesh and drinks his blood will have his life living within them and He will raise them up on the last day.

I want this as much for me as I do for my children. God loved me enough to send people into my life to help me find Him. Thank you, brothers and sisters in Christ, for helping me find the road of salvation and staying fixed on the race.

"So do not worry, saying, 'What shall we eat?' or 'What shall we drink?' or 'What shall we wear?' For the pagans run after all these things and your heavenly Father knows that you need them. But seek first his kingdom and his righteousness, and all these things will be given to you as well." (Matthew 6:31-33)

"Which of you, if his son asks for bread, will give him a stone? Or if he asks for a fish, will give him a snake? If you, then, though you are evil, know how to give good gifts to your children, how much more will your Father in heaven give good gifts to those who ask him!" *(Matthew 7: 9-11)*

Perfection is not a Requirement for Love

When Collin was four months old, he developed pneumonia and for the next four months was in and out of the hospital. Even when he was not in the hospital he was still very sick and I lived in great fear of losing him. I had to take him with me as I drove my other children to their events and saw to their needs, but in the back of my mind was always that concern I would hold him and pray, "Please Dear God, have mercy on us." While he was in the hospital, I would sit by his side and pray all the more. I pleaded for his healing. I wanted more than anything to take him home with me safe, sound and in the fullness of health.

Never in any of the darkest hours of parenting any of my children would I have thought, 'Well, that one is not perfect so it doesn't matter if they live or die, so I will just leave them alone and see what happens.' I could never think, "Well, I have to take care of my other children, so this one is not important," any more than I could say to my other children, "Well, Collin is sick so you will all have to fend for yourselves." Yet, I often thought that was God's opinion about me. For lots of reasons both good and bad, I did not trust or believe in my Father's love for me. I knew how horribly imperfect I was. If He showed me any mercy it would be out of pity and as an after-thought. I did not understand what I meant to him. I thought I should just fend for myself. While I would have braved any danger to keep my children safe with me, I never gave our Father in Heaven credit for having already done just that for me. When I was in my worse spiritual health, wavering on the brink of spiritual death, my Father in Heaven was holding me close, longing to restore me to complete health and bring me home safe and sound. And while others were having more troubles than I had, my Father in Heaven was still mindful of my needs.

We can never out do or out-love God who is all love. Created in His image, we cannot love our children more than he loves each and every one of us. He could no more forget us than we could forget our own children. Our names are written on his palm and He promised that even if our own mother and father should forget us, he will never forget us. It is impossible for Him to forget any one of us, for if it were possible for him to forget anyone of us, then He would simply not be God.

"What, then, shall we say in response to this? If God is for us, who can be against us?" *(Romans 8:31)*

The Bully

One afternoon, Ben came inside very upset from playing outside. One of the older neighbor boys had pushed him around. He fell and really scrapped up his knees. I bound up the wounds then went in search of the boy and his mother to talk with them. It doesn't take much for the mama bear to come out in me and that day was no different from any other. I was bound and determined to let that boy know he was not to touch or bother my child again. I flew to Ben's defense without a second thought.

That is why when I heard Joyce Meyers tell the same sort of story about her son and husband, I could really relate. Joyce explained that her husband, Dave, heard the fight outside. He did not go first to the refrigerator to check the chore list to see if his son had finished all his work. Nor did he look to see if there were any bad checks against his name for infractions during the week. No, instead he nearly tore the front door off the frame of the house going out to aid his son.

Our God does not weigh our sins against our good deeds to see if we are worthy of his loving concern. Our God does not dole out help to us out of some arrogant sense of pity. Our God is loving concern incarnate. He would do no less than we do to watch over and protect our children. When others come against us, we have but to stand in faith and wait as our God comes to our aid. When they attack us as we stand in faith, they come against God. I feel sorry for them because they never stood a chance. Like the snowball in the desert or the bucket against the tide, they will never prevail.

"He who dwells in the shelter of the Most High, will rest in the shadow of the Most High. I will say of the Lord, 'He is my refuge and my fortress, my God in whom I trust.

Surely He will save you from the fowler's snare, and from the deadly pestilence. He will cover you with his feathers and under his wings you will find refuge; his faithfulness will be your shield and rampart.

You will not fear the terror of the night, nor the arrow that flies by day, nor the pestilence that stalks in the darkness, nor the plague that ravages at midday.

A thousand may fall at your side, ten thousand at your right hand, but it will not come near you.

You will only observe with your eyes and see the punishment of the wicked." *(Psalm 91: 1 – 8)*

When Did You Learn To Lie To Me?

When Collin was little, he did not know how to lie to me. He would innocently tell me the truth, even when it might get him in trouble. In his innocence, he never understood how to try and save face or to cover his tracks. He did not have the pride to protect which would culminated in deceit. He did not understand that greed was wrong.

As he got older, he began to pass the blame to others. Suddenly, his Daddy or the dog took the cookies. He was sure of it. When this did not work, he would try to bluff his way out of it by pretending to not know how the problem may have occurred. Then in desperation, he would try to bully his way into freedom by demanding to know why it was so important in the first place. I would wait for it. Finally, the truth would come out. Yes, he was responsible. Yet, he still may not accept full responsibility as he made a pitiful plea that he just had to do it, he was hungry after all. At what point did he learn to lie to me? How did he begin this dance around the truth, doing everything except embrace it? When did he learn to hide the truth in darkness?

Even though we like to think of ourselves as mature adults, we all do the same thing. We rationalize every form of behavior and make excuses for it. We try every plan of self-defense known to man. And God has heard them all. Did we really think God would believe the lies? "The woman gave me the apple to eat." "The snake tricked me into eating it." As soon as we learn right from wrong, we suddenly begin to choose badly. We test the waters and set the bench mark. How fast over the limit can we drive before we are ticketed or worse yet hurt ourselves and others? "But I was in a hurry Officer." How many lies can we tell before we are caught in one? "What does it matter anyway?" How many nickels and dimes can we steal before we are stealing hundreds of dollars? "They are rich, they can afford it."

Every lie binds us to another until we are dragging around baggage nearly impossible to carry in complete darkness afraid that others will see them and know. Our Father gave us a way out. It is the truth that sets us free. Truth that may come with some very difficult and painful consequences. But it also gives relief to the heavy heart and the opportunity to start over without the weight of guilt. Being human, we may carry the guilt but Our Father offers us a way out of that too. Forgiveness. Then we can have true freedom. We just have to learn to embrace the truth, accept the consequences, ask for forgiveness and let go of the guilt. Your Father in heaven wants you to be free of all that holds you down and keeps you from being totally free of self-loathing and guilt. Embrace the truth.

"If you hold to my teachings, you are really my disciples. Then you will know the truth, and the truth will set you free." *(John 8:32)*

They Never Stood a Chance

Have you ever felt as if coming to work was preparing for battle? On those days, I must cover myself with prayer and pick up my shield of faith. As I drive up to the office, I have often said to the Lord, "Cover me Lord, I'm goin' in." It is wrong to believe that we face the war all by ourselves. God walks with us. When the evil comes at me to devour my flesh, my enemies themselves will stumble and fall. We are not alone.

When they come against us, they come against the Lord God. They never stood a chance. It is also wrong to think our conflict is with flesh and blood. And our victory is not in seeing our enemies destroyed, but in seeing those held captive by Satan freed from his grasp just as the Lord has freed us, so that we may celebrate together the victory of God over sin and death with all of our brothers and sisters in Christ.

"For our struggle is not against flesh and blood, but against the rulers, against the authorities: against the powers of this dark world; and against the spiritual forces of evil in the heavenly realms." *(Ephesians 6:12)*

How Much I Miss Them

It hit me like the proverbial ton of bricks the minute I had to end my phone call with my son, Ken, and my grandbaby, Henry. I realized how much I missed them and being with them especially on the holidays. My heart ached that I could not hold them. Talking with them was wonderful but not exactly like the gift of presence that I longed for. I missed my children who have now gone on with their lives and are living so far from home and I miss the time we had together. I pray they will know that no matter what happens or how far they travel or where they go, they can always come home. I think that God has given me this experience not just because it is a normal path of life but as a reminder that He longs for each of us in much the same way. Our prayers are nice, if they are like phone calls home, but so distant. What He longs for is the gift of our presence. Why else would He offer the awesome indwelling of His Holy Spirit within us?

God's promise is true. Jesus tells us, "If anyone loves me, he will obey my teaching. My Father will love him and we will come to him and make our home with him." *(John 14:23)* He reminds us that He will never leave us orphaned and alone. It is so good to know that we have our home with Him always and everywhere. He who never forgets us and never abandons us will always be present to us and for us.

Discipline of the Lord

When my father would discipline my brothers and me when we were little, he would say, 'this hurts me more than it hurts you.' I did not believe him. Then I had children and found out he was correct. Disciplining was the hardest tasks I had as a parent and it did hurt a lot. There were times when I would rather have gone through root canal surgery! I would have taken the punishment for them if it would have corrected their behavior. If my children were to have believed me when I said, 'It hurts me more than it hurts you,' it would have taken a lot of faith on their part. There were times when active punishment was necessary but there were times, just letting them suffer the results of their actions was sufficient.

I think a lot of the time, our Father in Heaven allows us to suffer the results of our bad decisions. I know one time when He had to get a hold of me in a way that I could not dispute his hand was heavy upon me for discipline. I had bargained with God to save me from that pit of despair. Then when He pulled me free, I allowed an evil influence to convince me I was stupid to believe in God. So I turned my back on him and denied him. My Father in Heaven got a hold of me much like you would grab a feral kitten, by the scruff of the neck and would not let go. I fought him for a week. I found out two things about my bargain with God. First, if you make a deal with God, you had better keep your end of the bargain. And secondly, a bargain is not a real relationship and a real relationship is what our Father truly wants with us. After a week, even my stubborn little soul could not hold out. I told him, 'OK, You Exist'. I felt him release his grip. But then being the snotty little kid I was, and needing to have the last word, I said, "BUT I am not going to believe in someone I don't know!" I fell right into his hands, for to know God is to love him. And so began the second, true conversion, based on a deep love for a Father who would not let go of me and on a faith in a loving Father who already sent his son to take the punishment for my sins. I am so grateful He did would not let go saying, 'This one is too much trouble'.

Father, did it hurt you more than it hurt me?

"My son, do not make light of the Lord's discipline and do not lose heart when He rebukes you, because the Lord disciplines those He loves, and He punishes everyone He accepts as a son." *(Hebrews 12:6)*

Come Out Of That Cave

I recently attended the convention for the International Fellowship of Christian Businessmen, in St. Louis, Missouri, and had the pleasure of hearing Don Allen speak. Don has a Christian Ministry on TV called, "Christ the Healer" and he said a few things that really touched my heart and challenged me.

In the story about the man who brings his son to Jesus for healing, he is distraught because Jesus's disciples could not heal his son. He tells Jesus that the boy is possessed and is often thrown into water and fire as if to kill the boy. He begs Jesus, that if he can, to please heal his son. Jesus replies, "If I can? With God, nothing is impossible."

Don said he reads that passage just a little differently. It is not just that there is nothing that is impossible for God to do, but to do nothing at all is impossible for God. God who promises to answer our prayers in faith, could never stand back and do nothing. Even when it seems that nothing is happening, God is there in our midst doing something. He is an ever present source of love and protection in the face of evil and disaster. He is a comforter and protector. Doing nothing is impossible for God.

The man was brought to his knees so to speak and responded to Jesus saying, "Lord, forgive my unbelief, increase my faith." I realized when Don said that, I was just like that man, unsure if God would act. I believed He heard my prayers, yet I lacked trust in him

115

to respond. Sometimes I feel as if I have lived a lot of my life inside a cave, hiding from all the turmoil around me, afraid to step out of the shadows and trust in the light. Like Elijah who was hiding in the cave when the windstorm ripped the mountain and the fire scorched the earth and the earthquake shook the ground beneath his feet. When the Lord came by, it was a still soft voice who asked Elijah, "Why are you here?"

The truth is, I let the world scare me into hiding and I do not always trust enough to step out in faith. It is about time to come out of that cave into the light and stop being afraid that God will do nothing if I cry out to him.

A Home Run

I had the pleasure of taking my son to a Cardinals baseball game recently. As we sat watching the game, he relaxed and put his head on my shoulder and enjoyed himself. It was not always an easy task taking Collin alone to a baseball game. I often discovered it was a very difficult task. He had a lot of issues that made it hard to take him anywhere. He would either get away from me or get scared at something and shut down or need to go to the bathroom every 15 minutes, or any one of a dozen of things that kept both of us from enjoying the game. It was not that he was being difficult on purpose, he just could not do any better. No matter how difficult it might be, it would never crossed my mind that I should just give up on him and never try to take him anywhere ever again or abandon him. When I see old documentaries of institutions of the past, where mothers and fathers were often told to send their disabled babies away and forget them, I cringe. My mind is filled with a stubborn anger and determination. "NOT MY BABY," cries my heart. We are in this game together and we will be here until it is time to go home. So if it got difficult, I would know that at least we tried and maybe next year would be better.

I did not realize it then because I had no idea if and when he might ever mature or improve. As he got older he learned to trust me that I would not just take him somewhere and abandon him. That I would stay with him through the entire game and look for him if he chose not

117

to stay with me. He could truly enjoy our time together whether our team was winning or losing. He could be reassured that I was right next to him and would provide for him. So, too, must my Father in Heaven look at me. How often must He have looked at me, hoping that I would learn to lean on him? But He continued to take me along to the game in hopes I will simply relax and enjoy it as I learn to trust Him and know that He will never abandon me, that He will stay with me and look for me if I get lost. For me, trust is a difficult issue. But if I can be more like Collin then maybe, just maybe, I can be the fullness of joy to Him who knows every hair on my head and has called me by name – the fullness of what I was created to be.

Nothing can compare to when Jesus hit the ball clear out of the park so high that it changed the course of human history and still revolves around the earth. That gift alone makes me one of the luckiest people on the earth. But there is one more thing that I know as well. Several of Collin's teachers once told us that Collin was very lucky to have us as his parents. They were wrong in a sense. I realized as I drove home from the game, that it was I who was lucky to have Collin. I am truly blessed. My Father in Heaven knew I needed someone to show me the way to home base.

"I have learned the secret of being content in any and every situation." *(Philippians 4:11)*

Mary and Collin

Those we love, teach us about God who is love. Write your own stories here.

Acknowledgements

Allen, Don. Keynote speaker for the 2015 Fellowship of Christian Businessmen in St. Louis, MO. 18 July 2015. Website *Two Guys and a Bible*. Copyright © 2013. <<u>www.twoguysandabible.com</u>>

Brophy, Don. *Catherine of Siena. A Passionate Life* New York, NY. Blue Bridge. 2010

Curious George. Dir. Matthew O'Callaghan. Writer: Ken Kaufmann, screen play. Based on the book, *Curious George* by Hans Augusto and Margret Rey. Perfs. Will Ferrell, Drew Barrymore, Eugene Levy. DVD. Universal Pictures, 2006.

International Fellowship of Christian Businessmen. Copyright © 2015. <<u>www.IFCB.org</u> >

Kolodiejchuk, Brian, *Mother Teresa, Come be My Light, The Private Writings of the "Saint of Calcutta"*, New York, USA, Doubleday 2007

Lucado, Max. *The Applause of Heaven*. Nashville, TN. Thomas Nelson Inc. 2008.

Joyce Meyer Ministries. Author, Teacher and Minister. Copyright © 2015 <<u>www.joycemeyer.org</u> >

Vanauken, Sheldon. *A Severe Mercy. A Story of Faith, Tragedy and Triumph*. Including 18 letters from C.S. Lewis. New York City, NY. Harper One. 1977.

Printed in the United States
By Bookmasters